If there were ever a writer who can wrest beauty out of deep complexity and pain, it is Amy Julia Becker. Written with elegant honesty, her new book explores the burden of privilege and the responsibility and call to steward it well. I'm grateful for Becker's willingness to wade into deep waters and to emerge from them with a timely vision of human flourishing for all.

KATELYN BEATY, author of *A Woman's Place: A Christian Vision for Your Calling in the Office, the Home, and the World*

Without shaming or victimizing, Becker considers painful truths and beautiful possibilities for healing the divisions of our present moment.

GABE LYONS, founder of Q Ideas

A deeply human book. As a woman who shares many of Becker's advantages, I've been immensely helped, by Becker's words, to begin believing that God can use our suffering—and our privilege—for good.

JEN POLLOCK MICHEL, author of *Teach Us to Want: Longing, Ambition and the Life of Faith*

Amy Julia Becker allows us to enter an important—but not easy—spiritual journey of awakening and enlightenment. Writing beautifully and elegantly in prose that does not allow us to shrink from a painful reality, Becker challenges us to move out of the stagnant state of "benign" racism. Without "white-explaining," Becker presents a convincing story of everyday privilege, a disruption of that privilege, and a necessary transformation.

SOONG-CHAN RAH, author of *Many Colors: Cultural Intelligence for a Changing Church*

I want to read every word Amy Julia Becker writes. No one else I know captures so completely the ache and the joy of being human. *White Picket Fences* is her most compelling book yet, tackling one of the thorniest topics of our time and illuminating it with honesty, humility, and hope. Privilege so often involves a conspiracy to forget, and this book gently, unflinchingly insists that we remember. But it also helps us believe that in a world so often torn by violence and indifference, love can still have the last and best word.

ANDY CROUCH, author of *Strong and Weak: Embracing a Life of Love, Risk, and True Flourishing*

Discussing the reality of privilege is both uncomfortable and essential. In *White Picket Fences*, Amy Julia Becker explores this critically important topic without being heavy-handed or didactic. I was pulled in from page 1 by Amy Julia's writing, which is warm, honest, and inviting as she beautifully explores her own life and story of privilege. Compelling, wise, and vital.

TISH HARRISON WARREN, author of *Liturgy of the Ordinary: Sacred Practices in Everyday Life*

As a white mother of black children, I find this topic to be nuanced and highly personal. Amy Julia masterfully created a safe space for my heart to explore what has otherwise felt like a loaded subject. This is a book for every thoughtful soul.

SARA HAGERTY, author of *Unseen: The Gift of Being Hidden in a World That Loves to Be Noticed*

Renouncing privilege isn't always possible—or even desirable. In *White Picket Fences*, Amy Julia enters this conversation with wisdom and candor, inviting the reader to consider the transforming power of grace and gratitude to direct what we've been given to do the work of love.

RACHEL MARIE STONE, author of *Birthing Hope: Giving Fear to the Light*

A writer of beauty, bravery, and compassion takes on a topic as searingly painful as it is depressingly timely. As she shares her own journey so unsparingly, Becker nudges readers toward self-reflection, inspiring hope for new beginnings and opening hearts to healing.

RACHEL SIMON, author of *Riding the Bus with My Sister: A True Life Journey*

Through Amy Julia's raw and vulnerable storytelling, I discovered not only the harm my own privilege has caused but also a God-birthed desire to actively engage in reconciliation and healing. Captivating and deeply personal, *White Picket Fences* is Amy Julia's best work yet.

JEANNIE CUNNION, author of *Mom Set Free: Find Relief from the Pressure to Get It All Right*

It takes a special kind of writer—a special kind of person—to write about privilege in a vulnerable way. Amy Julia Becker is exactly such a writer and such a person. Becker offers an unflinching examination of what obligations and obstacles come with privilege in a world marred by so many injustices done to those without the advantages many of us take for granted. *White Picket Fences* is a must-read for all who wish to break down the barriers that divide our communities and our nation today.

KAREN SWALLOW PRIOR, author of *On Reading Well: Finding the Good Life through Great Books*

White Picket Fences bravely confronts privilege whilst challenging readers to do the same. As Becker gets personal with her reader, she offers more than perceived answers: She offers space and grace. At a time when allies continue to peel back the layers of privilege in their lives, *White Picket Fences* is timely!

CAROLINA HINOJOSA-CISNEROS, Tejana poet and freelance writer

White Picket Fences sparks conversations that promote mutual compassion and respect as Becker celebrates the diversity and intrinsic value of all people. With a watchword of *hope*, Becker inspires readers to bridge our divides united as a community, strengthened by the Lord, shielded with prayer, and armed with love.

XOCHITL E. DIXON, Our Daily Bread Ministries

Both an excellent primer for entering the conversation and an invitation to change, as told through the art of story, with generous amounts of grace. I have no doubt that Becker's book will help steer a much-needed dialogue of examining our own stories and entering into repentance.

CARA MEREDITH, author of *The Color of Life: A White Woman's Journey toward Love and Justice*

Amy Julia Becker puts poignant and powerful words around a subject that is sensitive but so necessary to discuss, perhaps now more than ever. In our hyperconnected yet increasingly siloed world, we need personal, humble, and openhanded conversations like *White Picket Fences* to help us on this path of healing and flourishing together.

KATHERINE AND JAY WOLF, coauthors of *Hope Heals: A True Story of Overwhelming Loss and Overcoming Love*

Amy Julia Becker is opening herself up to being raked over. She doesn't have to do it. Nevertheless, she doesn't shy away from the good, bad, and ugly of her privileged upbringing. Gentle and beautiful, this book is hard-hitting.

MARLENA GRAVES, author of *A Beautiful Disaster: Finding Hope in the Midst of Brokenness*

WHITE PICKET FENCES

turning toward love in a world divided by privilege

amy julia becker

A NavPress resource published in alliance with Tyndale House Publishers, Inc.

NavPress is the publishing ministry of The Navigators, an international Christian organization and leader in personal spiritual development. NavPress is committed to helping people grow spiritually and enjoy lives of meaning and hope through personal and group resources that are biblically rooted, culturally relevant, and highly practical.

For more information, visit www.NavPress.com.

White Picket Fences: Turning toward Love in a World Divided by Privilege

A NavPress resource published in alliance with Tyndale House Publishers, Inc.

The Team:
Don Pape, Publisher
David Zimmerman, Acquisitions Editor
Elizabeth Symm, Copy Editor
Dean H. Renninger, Designer

The author is represented by Foundry Literary + Media.

Cataloging-in-Publication Data is available.

ISBN 978-1-63146-920-6

Printed in the United States of America

24 23 22 21 20 19 18
7 6 5 4 3 2 1

For Mom and Dad

You gave me what I needed to ask these questions

and to begin to find the answers.

Thank you.

The discovery of our common humanity, beneath our differences, seems for many to be dangerous. It not only means that we have to lose some of our power, privilege, and self-image, but also that we have to look at the shadow side in ourselves, the brokenness, and even the evil in our own hearts and culture; it implies moving into a certain insecurity.

JEAN VANIER, *BECOMING HUMAN*

Contents

foreword

Strangers at the Gate

I first met Amy Julia Becker in a classic "privilege" moment. She was an editor. I was a writer. I am black. She is white. We'd never met, not even on paper. I hadn't read her books. She hadn't read mine. In the sticky potential of this power dynamic, my concern was immediate and race-based. Would she, as a white woman, tread lightly over my precious (as I saw them) and hard-wrought words? Or would she grab my topic and slash and burn? My humble article was on race relations, and her audience that murky November—just a few short months after Michael Brown was gunned down and killed in Ferguson, Missouri—was mostly white. I am black, indeed. And these times are tough and rugged.

In the midst of the push and pull, Amy Julia was faced with agreeing, as literary icon James Baldwin said of writing, that "the point is to get your work done, and your work is to change the world."[1] Or as George Orwell, author of the classic novel *1984*, observed of his writing: "When I sit down to write a book, I do not say to myself, 'I am going to produce a work of art.' I write it because there is some lie that I want to expose, some fact to which I want to draw attention, and my initial concern is to get a hearing."[2]

This can be scary stuff—seeking to bend the universe with a few trembling words. Thus, my initial anxiety about Amy Julia was this: Would she lay down the editor's pen long enough to hear my side? Or, rushing, would she tone down its arguments? Send back my essay covered in ink? Reject the piece outright, saying it wouldn't appeal to or address her audience?

None of that happened. Instead, as I discovered, Amy Julia asked the right questions. Next, she listened. Then she reflected. *Then* she made one suggestion: Weave in a little more faith. That was all she sought from me, her writer. A little more Jesus. But not with a heavy hand. She allowed me to point to Christ in a Matthew 14:27 sort of way: "Take courage. I am here!" (NLT). And for her, that was the ticket. Just enough.

In her, therefore, I found a brave combination of many things I respect not just in writers and editors, but in all people: namely, restraint, fairness, intelligence, curiosity, kindness, courage, hope. Over the next two years, as our paths continued to intersect, eventually she became the most important thing—a friend.

That is who you'll discover in *White Picket Fences*. It's an extraordinary book not because it's so urgent, which it is, or because it's profoundly well written—also undeniably true. You'll also discover Amy Julia, however, in fellowship, because this book is offered in the spirit of a welcoming traveler, someone wrestling with universal life issues—life and death and everything in between—but all examined through the lens of what, ironically, is called privilege.

The concept, in these times, raises hackles and seething defenses. Draped in the sound of something grand—*privilege*—it has become not a positive idea, but politically charged to a fault. Mention "privilege" to some who enjoy it and they recoil, defenses raging.

Amy Julia asks readers to hold the noise—to consider the hard reality that, in a society, "privilege harms everyone, those who are excluded from it and those who benefit from it." Even more, she asks readers to widen their lens on privilege—to look at race, yes, but to wrestle beyond race matters to explore the privilege of physical ability, gender, economic status, birthplace, education, and more.

As a mother of a child with Down syndrome, Amy Julia displayed her capacity to examine the heart and soul of such spiritual struggles in her book *A Good and Perfect Gift: Faith, Expectations, and a Little Girl Named Penny*—named one of the Top Books of 2011 by *Publishers Weekly*.

With *White Picket Fences*, she moves again into tough territory—first asking white people who are skittish about race to take a leap of faith and trust her enough to fully examine their own privilege, even if their very sense of self is broken up and rebuilt in the process. Then she invites the rest of us to build alongside, not sitting idly by and quiet, but affirming her right to add to the ongoing conversation about these national matters—because every voice is needed. No matter when that voice enters the room.

As she says: "I want this story to open up the conversations we are afraid to have, to prompt the questions we are afraid to ask, and to lead us away from fear and toward love, in all its fragile and mysterious possibilities."

Is this indulgent writing? When *un*privileged folks are getting gunned down in the streets—by civil servants hired to protect them?

In fact, it's the kind of writing encouraged by researcher Dr. Peggy McIntosh, the scholar credited with affirming the problems of white privilege in 1988.[3] Taking a hard look at her privileged life as a white, Ivy League academic, McIntosh observed that

> My schooling followed the pattern . . . [that] whites are taught to think of their lives as morally neutral, normative, and average, and also ideal, so that when we work to benefit others, this is seen as work that will allow "them" to be more like "us."[4]

Fearless to expose this tension, McIntosh then called for more transparency:

> We need more down-to-earth writing by people about these taboo subjects. We need more understanding of the ways in which white "privilege" damages white people, for these are not the same ways in which it damages the victimized.[5]

The privilege conundrum is not a neutral matter, to be sure.

Yanked from the academic sphere and into our everyday lingo, privilege demands to be examined from all sides in our culture, and in brave ways. Not with denial but with determination, and also with guts. Amy Julia Becker decided to rise to the challenge and take on urgent questions: *If I'm privileged, and that hurts the people who aren't, what can we all do about it? What, indeed, is God asking us to do? And how, personally, do I prepare myself to help offer answers?*

The result is the story of her journey to try and figure it all out.

And here's the thing: Her story is beautiful and it is right.

I say that as an African American woman, even though I don't agree with every single conclusion that Amy Julia makes. She and I went back and forth on when to tell children about hard things such as racism. I argued that the question itself is a luxury allotted to children who don't have to worry about this particular terror—while children of color, by default, are forced to see from their earliest months that they are targets, often, of many kinds of racism.

Thus, all children, I argued, should see that racial terror exists—just as they're taught that a stove is hot, a speeding car can kill them, and sadly, so can other mayhem. Racism kills, too, and all children, no matter how young, should know about it. Then they can become justice allies and advocates, no matter how young.

I write those words in my own rush to fix a broken world,

forgetting theologian Richard Foster's wry and wise reminder to "lay down the everlasting burden of always needing to manage others" or, indeed, to "set others straight."[6]

Watching Amy Julia wrestle with such matters helped me acknowledge one hard reality of the privilege coin. Everybody has a viewpoint, and it's critical to hear it, even if every view doesn't line up with my own. Yet, if we're listening, that means we are talking to each other. Or getting closer to it.

That's what Amy Julia did with me and many others as she wrote this book. She shared, listened, reflected, and replied. Now she asks the same of readers. Allow her to talk about the privilege problem. But don't stop there. Talk back.

As she acknowledges at the book's ending, she's not an expert with all of the answers. Instead: "I am one vulnerable, distractible, self-centered human being trying to come to terms with the gifts and sorrows of my life. It will take thousands upon thousands of others who are willing to do the same, to bow our knees and take up a posture of humility, of listening to others instead of insisting on hearing our own voices, of admitting our own complicity in harm, of opening our hands and hearts to healing even when it hurts."

To weigh our own stories, therefore, consider hers. It's the least any writer asks. Turn the page and read. And with tough topics, here's the thing. The journey is beautiful. And it is right.

Patricia Raybon

Introduction

My left eyelid flutters, a tiny movement, an unpredictable and intermittent distraction, like a fly that buzzes and twirls and lands with an abrupt stop, only to take flight again. Then the right eyelid joins in, sometimes playing a solo, sometimes in a cacophony of motion, as if competing with its pair. After a few weeks, the twitch settles into my right eye, persistent and uncontrollable.

I don't wear glasses. My eyes have never twitched before. I think I must be spending too much time in front of the computer, but sometimes my eye will twitch when I'm not staring at a screen, and sometimes I spend hours replying to email without any twitching. Eventually, I notice a pattern. The twitch surfaces whenever I am working on, or even thinking about, this book.

I mention this minor affliction to a friend.

"I think you're flinching," she says.

I think she might be right. It seems possible that my subconscious mind has been imagining all the critical words that could be flung my way if anyone pays attention to the stories and arguments and hopes inside these pages. It is as if I am already ducking and taking cover. It is also as if I am afraid of what I might see if I keep my eyes open.

After my friend's assessment, every time the twitch returns I close my eyes, take a deep breath, and say to myself, "I am safe." Then I pray, "Protect me."

That very day, the twitching slows, and within a few more days, it is gone.

Apparently, my body wanted to send an alert, to help me recognize the fear I feel as an affluent, able-bodied white woman trying to address topics like race and class and disability. What surprises me is that the twitching doesn't stop because I conquer my fears. It stops because I decide to keep my eyes open even though I am afraid.

I am afraid that in writing this book, I will look at my life and come face to face with truths I don't want to see about myself. I am afraid I will criticize the very people who have given me the safe and stable neighborhoods I have enjoyed, the education that has opened doors for learning and growth, and the religious faith that has anchored my soul. I am also afraid that I will mount a defense of myself and of the individuals and systems that have brought me here, and that I might do so without regard for the people who have been cut off from the neighborhoods and schools and opportunities I have known. And finally, I am afraid of exposing the darker sides of privilege, afraid of what I might see when confessing the ways wealth and power wound others and the ways they wound the wealthy and powerful.

This book tells a story of my growing awareness not only that I have received unwarranted benefits by virtue of my white skin, Protestant heritage, and able body, but also that these unwarranted benefits have done harm to me and to others. In an era of political division, concerns over the plight of immigrants and the working class, movements like Occupy Wall Street and Black Lives Matter, and news reports about police brutality against people of color, I am not alone in confronting my place within these systems and seeing pain there. I join these other voices with hope that exposing the pain can lead to healing.

But healing is not easy.

Last winter, I spent a few days in Florida with my husband. We decided to take a walk through downtown Miami, so I put on my flip-flops for the first time since summer. By the end of our walk, the top of my feet had become a line of blisters underneath the leather straps of the flip-flops, oozing and raw. In the morning, I couldn't put on my shoes without wincing. Over the next two weeks, the blisters scabbed over, and the pain turned to irritation. As the new skin grew, as these minor wounds healed, the itching even interrupted my sleep. My whole body squirmed from the discomfort of growing new skin.

Recognizing the advantages of my position as a white woman has been a little bit like waking up in the middle of the night with those blisters. The analogy works only on a superficial level: Acknowledging my own privilege has exposed wounds that already existed, and the pain from wearing flip-flops is absurd in comparison to the depth of injury human beings have inflicted upon one another in our efforts to gain advantages and prestige. But that visceral response to the work of healing—the fact that my whole body paid uncomfortable attention as the new skin grew—makes it seem like an appropriate comparison for the concept of healing on a cultural level. In recent years, I've become aware not only that privilege exists—that laws have been written throughout US history to protect and support certain groups of people, people like me, at the expense of others—but also that privilege operates in predictable, soothing, and ultimately harmful ways. Identifying the wounds of privilege is one thing, and an uncomfortable one in and of itself. Participating in their healing is even harder. I hold out hope that wholeness lies on the other side of the discomfort, even if the scars of the past remain.

Our three children were born to two white, wealthy, educated people. They were born into privilege. Our oldest daughter, Penny, was also diagnosed with Down syndrome shortly after she was born. She was born into a set of genetic and social disadvantages over which she had no control. When Penny was two years old, I was looking for a preschool program for a few mornings a week. I called one that had been recommended by a friend. I talked with the director and explained that our daughter had Down syndrome. She cut me off before I could say anything more. "We wouldn't be able to accommodate your daughter," she said. I didn't fight back. I just hung up the phone, disoriented, angry, and with a taste of being excluded from consideration because of what category my child fit into, rather than based upon who she was as an individual.

Penny's situation heightened my awareness of negative assumptions and social barriers I had never encountered before. Throughout the past decade, I have begun to see that I am insulated from many of the obstacles faced by the rest of our society, not only when it comes to disability but also when it comes to both racial and socioeconomic disparities. What's more, I have woken up to the call for justice and mercy and healing throughout the history and Scripture of my faith tradition. As a Christian, as a mother, as an affluent white woman who has struggled with seasons of worry and sadness and long stretches of drinking too much wine, I want to participate in human connection instead of division, in healing instead of further harm.

I err easily on the side of utopianism. I grew up with an ability to trust institutions and authority figures because they rewarded me for playing by their rules, and I still tend to think every problem can be solved through hard work and a positive attitude. But wrestling with a fractured national identity, with the divisions of race and class and ability (not to mention gender and nationality and sexuality and political affiliation, though those topics extend beyond the scope of this book), has humbled me. I have started to see that the only adequate response to the ruptures within our culture is a mutual one, one in which disparate groups of people are willing to work together.

Most of the time, being white and affluent and educated puts me in a position of strength, but in looking for ways that our culture might heal, I find myself in a position of weakness. The only way healing can happen is if the people who have been excluded and marginalized are willing to forgive and trust people like me.

I have come to believe that privilege harms everyone, those who are excluded from it and those who benefit from it. I want this book to be an invitation, especially for people from a cultural background similar to mine, to consider the reality of privilege, the benefits and wounds that come from privilege, and whether we can respond to the fact of our privilege with generosity, humility, and hope. I am not claiming to be an expert, nor am I trying to prescribe action steps for individuals or communities. I want this story to open up the conversations we are afraid to have, to prompt the questions we are afraid to ask, and to lead us away from fear and toward love, in all its fragile and mysterious possibilities.

chapter one

LIFE IS A GIFT

I only hear her speak Spanish. We lie side by side in the hospital, a white curtain pulled tight between us. I never see her face. I see the scuffed sneakers and blue jeans of the kids who I assume are her older children. I hear the cadence of their voices and pick out words I learned years ago: *Hola, Mamá . . . Tranquila . . . ¡Qué linda!*

We have both just given birth at Yale New Haven Hospital, and we are lodged here together temporarily, until private rooms open up. I am warm and exhilarated and grateful, as if waves of light are pouring over me. Marilee lies in my arms, bundled and asleep. Peter has stepped out to buy lunch and to greet my mother when she arrives with our older children, Penny and William. I gaze out the window on my side of the room. The barren winter landscape stands in direct opposition to my emotions—the gray sky looks almost white with cold, the gray water of Long Island Sound lies flat in the distance.

A midwife comes in, one I haven't met before. She has short brown hair, and her whole body looks efficient: shirt tucked in, clipboard in hand, glasses pushed firmly in place on her nose. "This is your third child?"

I smile down at Marilee's round face and murmur, "Yes."

"Have you considered an IUD?" she asks. Something in her tone puts me on alert.

"Um," I say, "no, I haven't."

"Do you use contraception?" I can't tell if she is bored or annoyed.

"All three of my pregnancies were planned, if that's what you're asking," I say.

"Well, you might want to consider an IUD. It would protect you from pregnancy for five years, though it wouldn't protect you from sexually transmitted diseases."

I feel like a little kid receiving a reprimand for breaking a rule I hadn't known to obey. Her eyes seem to narrow into a glare. I glance down at Marilee's peaceful face again, take a deep breath, and remind myself that I have done nothing wrong in bringing this child into the world.

"Thank you for the information," I say.

As if we were in a standoff and she has conceded, she nods with a quick bob of her head, turns on her heel, and leaves.

An orderly comes in to move me to a different room a few minutes later, and soon after that, Penny and William peek around the doorframe to see their baby sister for the first time. William, two and a half, wears a button-down shirt and a charcoal gray sweater, his face stern with the responsibility of touching his sister's cheek. Penny, who has just turned five, kisses Marilee's feet again and again, her eyes wide, her face holding a perpetual smile at the excitement of a new member of the family. They bring cupcakes and we all sing "Happy Birthday" to their new baby sister.

After they go home with my mother, I review the day in my mind, as if replaying the events of the past twenty-four hours will cement them in my memory. I think back to the contraction that woke me at 3 a.m., the call to my aunt and uncle to stay with the kids until Mom could arrive. I trace the route to the hospital, the dark empty streets, the serious expression on Peter's face with both hands on the steering wheel, the reminder to myself to breathe. The pain of labor and delivery has already become imprecise, a rivet of hardship filled in by the sweetness, the joy, the embrace, the blessing, yes, the blessing of Marilee's bare body curled upon my chest, her breathing steady, her eyes closed. Today was the third time I have given birth. With Penny, the nurses swaddled her and handed her to me, but soon took her out of my arms for testing. Two hours later, the doctors diagnosed her with Down syndrome, and the warmth and light of her birth seeped away, replaced, for a time, by fear. With William, I was so depleted from the all-night struggle to bring him into this world that I didn't have the strength to hold him. But with Marilee, there is no drama. We lie together, content, skin against skin. Blessing.

I move in my memory from the delivery room to the temporary room with the woman speaking Spanish from the bed behind the curtain. I will never see her again, but I feel connected to her. Our children share a birthday. Our bodies share the knowledge of intensity and wonder and welcome. Although I do not even know her name, I try to imagine her life. I conjure up a person based on an incongruous amalgamation of her kind voice and the statistics I have read about the city's Hispanic population. Peter is a graduate student at Yale right now, and I know from his remarks that the public schools in the city are struggling, that the poverty rate is high, that unemployment is high as well. I have read university security warnings about gunshots a few blocks from the campus and incidents of theft and sexual assault and murder.

I wonder if this woman's story fits into the demographic picture the reports have painted. How many children does she have? What kind of home are they living in? Would she welcome the news of an IUD, or would it come to her as an affront, a suggestion of incompetence or irresponsibility, as it had to me? My doctor later tells me that city hospitals make a point of talking with women about permanent birth control as soon as they've gone through labor. It helps avoid unwanted pregnancies, abortions, the financial distress of too many mouths to feed. *It wasn't a conversation designed with you in mind*, my doctor says.

Marilee's life stretches out in front of me. I know from experience the tedium that will come—the cries that cannot be comforted, the sleep that cannot be restored, the toenails to cut and diapers to change and the constant attentiveness required. But right now, the future is a promise—the wonder of discovering who this little person is becoming, of hearing her giggle for the first time, of watching her eyes follow her big brother and sister around the room, of feeling her soft breath and holding her close in the middle of the night, of swaying and rocking and giving of myself for her comfort, her peace.

I don't know the details yet—that Marilee will grow up to be my barefoot girl, the one who will toss her shoes and socks to the side even when the ground is frozen, or that she will have the gift of hospitality, always looking for ways to welcome a stranger into our midst. I do not know that she will spread her arms wide and rock her whole body with exuberance in the face of the smallest joys, or that her skin will become splotchy with hives after she experiences grief for the first time. I do not know that she will come up with a nickname for me, Mossy, or that the bridge of her nose will be covered with freckles in the summer, or that she will have trouble sitting still. But I know that her particular life is a gift, just like all the other babies born here today.

It comes across as a trite saying, a cliché: Every life is a gift. It prompts the questions I first asked in late-night conversations as a teenager: What about the lives that come into the world unwanted? What about the poor, the medically fragile, the refugee, the mentally ill—the lives that take up a disproportionate amount of time, money, attention? What about the ones like Penny, the ones who may never live independently, who may never participate through production in our consumer economy?

On the night Penny was born, when the contours of the future had become blurred by her diagnosis, a nurse came into the room. Peter's breathing had slowed as he slept in the pullout chair next to me. But I lay on my side, vaguely sore, replaying the events of the day. The nurse, an African American woman with a sturdy frame, said, "I had a special child too."

I made eye contact. "How old is your child now?"

"He died a long time ago," she said. Her voice stayed peaceful, but I felt the flutter of panic inside my chest. Her words named the very loss that terrified me.

"I'm sorry," I said, swallowing hard.

She shook her head, as if I didn't understand. "He was a gift," she said. And then she turned and left the room.

It took years for me to receive the truth of her simple statement. She wasn't saying he was a gift in spite of his needs. Or he was a gift in spite of his death. *He was a gift*. Pure and simple. Like the orphaned child and the premature baby and the little girl who will go to foster care tomorrow. Like the baby born to wealthy investment bankers. Like the baby born into poverty. Like Penny. Like William. Like Marilee, this little girl breathing so quickly and peacefully, heart pumping with the ferocity of life, eyelids fluttering, pink lips opening ever so slightly. A gift.

A hospital volunteer knocks and enters. We need to fill out forms—one for her birth certificate, Marilee Fuller Becker. Another to decline official photographs from the hospital's photographer. Another to review the experience—the check-in procedure, the nursing staff's demeanor, the décor of the room, the food. And then she gives me a book. It is a board book with a red cover, with what look like cutout bunnies on front. "This is for you and your baby," the lady says. "As a part of an early literacy program we've started." She hands me one more piece of paper. "If you fill this out, we'll send you another book when she turns one."

I overthink it: We have dozens, if not hundreds of books at home. We don't need this organization to spend money on us. But I believe in what they're offering me here. I want to applaud the effort, to demonstrate to donors that new mothers will welcome any support we are given to teach our children. I fill out the form, shaking my head at my ability to turn everything into a problem.

I think again about the woman from the bed next to mine, and I wonder how I would feel if our roles were reversed. I don't know if she only speaks Spanish, but it was the only language I heard, so I assume Spanish feels most natural to her. If I were raising my children in a different country, what would it feel like for me to try to read a picture book out loud? Perhaps they offer these books in Spanish, but I wonder—Would this mother be able to read this book to her baby? Would the words feel unfamiliar on her tongue?

We read to Penny and William most nights before bed, and I always think of those books as a bridge, a point of connection to other times and places and peoples. But, at the moment, this book feels like a wall, a subtle construction that separates me as a mother from the mother in the bed next door, like the curtain that separated us from seeing each other's faces. It is easy for me to read to my children. Easy for me to delight in the words, with my college degree in English literature. Easy for me to pass the building blocks for reading along to my children before they even go to school. Will the gift of one book do anything to help a mother in need?

I am well on my way to pitying this anonymous woman when I remember that five years earlier, when Penny was born, I was the mother in need. My college education and white skin and financial security did nothing to prepare me for the news that our daughter had Down syndrome. If anything, those marks of my social position brought with them unacknowledged expectations that life would be easier for us. I had never realized how wealth and education and all the unspoken benefits that accompany whiteness stood as barriers against Penny's diagnosis, walls that I thought protected me from vulnerability, from suffering, from discomfort, from fear, walls that kept me from understanding that life is both fragile and full of beauty in all its forms.

With the words *Down syndrome*, we moved from a category of self-sufficient parents into a category of parents eligible for significant social support. We needed far more than a program offering us a book. We needed therapists and specialized doctors and, eventually, public preschool with specialized teachers. We also needed friends and family and a church community to pray for us and bring us dinners and rejoice that our daughter—our needy, vulnerable, beautiful daughter—had been born. That web of support, from individuals to community organizations to state programs, held us up and eventually helped us move from a place of fear and sorrow to a place of joy. We were given what we needed to care for Penny, to see her thrive, even. She learned sign language. She learned to walk. She charmed everyone she encountered with her big eyes, her wide smile, and her habitual happy greeting—a wave and a breathy exclamation of "Hi!"

Marilee wriggles in my arms and interrupts my memories. Her little mouth puckers even though her eyes stay closed tight. I lift her toward my breast and begin the awkward attempt to feed her. My womb contracts as she suckles for a few minutes and falls asleep. The pain in my abdomen persists, and as much as I wish I didn't need to endure it, I also marvel at the way nourishing this little one is part of putting my body back together again, part of the painful, restorative act of healing. I nudge her awake but soon she sleeps again.

Just a few months earlier, when I was pregnant, I wrote an article for the *New York Times* parenting blog about my decision not to screen for Down syndrome with this third pregnancy. I had a higher chance of having another baby with Down syndrome, but our experience with Penny and other people with disabilities had convinced us that we would gratefully receive any child we were given. When I explained my reasoning in print, the comments poured in. Many came as affirmations of the path we had chosen. But many people criticized my decision. They even chastised me for it. To bring a child with Down syndrome into the world, some wrote, was unethical, in light of the suffering the condition would bring to the child, the burden it would place on the child's family, and the cost society would have to bear.

I hand Marilee to Peter and shift slowly to the side of the bed. My body is still bleeding. My flesh is still filled with fluid and fat and nutrients intended to sustain her life. I shuffle to the bathroom, my mind lingering on the responses to the *New York Times* article, to all those who wrote that it would be better not to have people with disabilities among us. This utilitarian logic used to make a certain amount of sense to me. Now I see it as a mirage. Like any utopian vision of independence and autonomy and health and happiness for all, it exists only as long as we eliminate the lives that involve need. As long as we prevent weakness from entering the world. But to eliminate weakness is to eliminate us all. Penny has helped me to recognize my own neediness, my own limitations, my own humanity. And she has helped me begin to see that even the people most different from me have gifts to offer.

I glance in the bathroom mirror. The harsh light draws attention to the dark lines under my eyes, my pasty skin, my unplucked eyebrows, and my dreary hair pulled back in a ponytail. I smile at myself. *Every life is a gift*, I think.

Penny has introduced me to the lives and stories of countless others with intellectual disabilities, hundreds of thousands, millions, the world over. I used to think a satisfying life of purpose was available only to people like me—self-sufficient, intellectual, able-bodied, affluent people. I have started to see that a satisfying and purposeful life is available to all, especially once we recognize our need for one another. As I slowly make my way toward the bed, I think back to the time a teenager with Down syndrome sat with William—my fussy, colicky baby boy—and with her calm presence brought more peace to his body than I had ever seen before. Or to my friend Elisa, whose daughter with an intellectual disability helps time slow down in their family as she walks through their days with gratitude and peace instead of busyness and anxiety.[1] I remember people I have read about over the years—the seminary students who live with adults with intellectual disabilities and grow to love and serve one another, the mother who writes about the profound wisdom and beauty of her adult child who needs constant physical care, the testimony of men like Jean Vanier or Henri Nouwen, who lived among people with Down syndrome and received gifts of love and acceptance they had never encountered elsewhere.

These stories leave me confident that even the individuals who appear broken by social standards are no more or less broken than I am, no more or less capable of contributing to our world, even if people like me have never learned to value their gifts. The inability to recognize that value is a failure on my part—a failure of imagination and of vision. When I refuse to see myself as sharing my humanity with people with Down syndrome, with people whose bodies function differently than my own, with people of a different ethnicity or skin color or socioeconomic status, I cut myself off from seeing my own need. As I weave a web of invulnerability, I cut myself off from allowing others to love me. The logic of self-sufficiency is a logic of loneliness. I understand the pragmatic argument that life with an intellectual disability is a burden to the self and the society, but I have begun to see that reasoning for what it is—a barren landscape, a desert.

I settle back into bed and turn to Peter, who stands by the window, gazing at Marilee. She looks so fragile in his arms. So many things could harm her. But the reason we could bring her into the world without prenatal screening tests and without fear is not because we believed she had won some cosmic genetic lottery and we were assured of a strong and healthy child. It is because we have learned that love—in all its vulnerability and need—is stronger than fear. That while some people judge Penny's life, most welcome her. That her doctors and teachers care for her with delight. That strangers and friends haven't retreated from us, but instead have been drawn near through Penny's welcoming presence as much as through their own willingness to receive her.

If I could go back to myself as a new mother holding her newborn baby and hearing the words *Down syndrome* and crying and feeling the fight of fear and love inside her chest, I would tell that frightened mother to trust her love. To trust that love will always be stronger than fear.

Now, fear has receded, leaving only a trace of its presence, like a line of seaweed after the tide flows out. Love remains.

I hold Marilee close. And I whisper to myself—and to the women who have given birth today, and to those struggling to conceive a child, and especially to those who have given birth to babies who are premature, or poor, or diagnosed with a disability—I whisper the truth that can so easily become muffled in a world of suffering. All of life is fragile and uncertain. All of life is beautiful and valuable. All of life is a gift.

chapter two

MIRRORS AND DOORS

Marilee comes home from the hospital in an ice storm. She also comes home on her father's birthday, and later, when he says, "You were my birthday present!" she responds, "Did I come home in a box?" envisioning herself amidst tissue paper, with a big pink satin bow ready to be untied.

In the two years following Marilee's birth, we move from Connecticut back to Peter's teaching job in New Jersey and then to an unexpected new job for Peter as the headmaster of a small coed boarding school in western Connecticut. The position comes with a house, but the house needs major renovations, and a rental property isn't available immediately, so we move four times in eight months. I don't have many friends in our new town. Peter is floating on excitement from the work ahead of him while I am submerged in my own exhaustion and bitterness over moving too often and working too little and wiping too many bottoms and waking up regularly to find four-year-old William demanding iPad time before the sun has come up. We find a church in town, but I give up on praying. I don't make time to exercise. I pity myself. I call it "the year of wine and nachos," a year marked by loneliness and anger and regret.

It is a season of discontent, but one source of stability comes from our nightly reading routine. The ritual goes like this: Marilee falls asleep in her crib. Penny and William don pajamas, brush teeth, use the potty, and scramble onto the love seat in the corner of their bedroom. Peter or I sit in the middle, Penny on one side and William on the other. The two children press against us, their soft warmth a comfort. Right now, William and I argue about many things—getting dressed, watching television, clearing his plate from the table. I find myself short-tempered with Penny most days too—she insists on the "special" blue cup at dinner even though William also wants it, or she lies on her bed instead of putting on her pants in the morning, and somehow those little acts of defiance feel like impossible obstacles to our day together. But when we sit down to read, there are no topics to argue about, no commands to issue, no negotiations over how many bites of broccoli must be consumed. It is predictable and comforting, and it holds us together.

Tonight we are reading Roald Dahl's *Charlie and the*

Chocolate Factory. I fold laundry on the bed as Peter settles between the children and resumes the story. Penny and William giggle at the escapades Mr. Wonka puts the children through. Peter wonders, with amusement in his voice, "Are we ever self-centered or overly focused on the television or inclined to eat too many sweets?" Penny and William look up at him with earnest faces, perhaps a little concerned that they might succumb to one of Mr. Wonka's punishments for selfishness. They see the traces of a smile, and they giggle again.

I stack the folded clothes in the basket, and the kids shuffle toward their beds—Penny on the left, under a pink comforter with white polka dots, William on the right, under a blue one with white stars. Peter kisses them good night, and then I sit down to sing. The kids request Christmas carols long after December has come and gone, so tonight I cycle through "Hark the Herald Angels Sing." The words are so familiar by now I don't even have to think about them. As I sing, my eyes rest on the bookshelf, this repository of memories and hopes and dreams. We've already read a few volumes from The Chronicles of Narnia, and we finished *The Cricket in Times Square* and *The Trumpet of the Swan*. I smile at the thought of introducing them to *Mrs. Piggle Wiggle* and *Little House on the Prairie* and *Pippi Longstocking*. I sit next to Penny, rubbing my thumb against the soft skin on the top of her hand. I usually leave the room before she has fallen asleep, but tonight I am wistful, grateful, happy to ignore the rush of tasks I could accomplish before my own bedtime.

I scan the books again—two shelves worth of classics. There are Thornton Burgess stories about animals in the forest and British novels like *The Little Princess* and *The Secret Garden*. Someday we will read about Anne Shirley, the orphan girl in *Anne of Green Gables* with her big, bold, kind heart, and about Jo March from *Little Women,* with her headstrong passion and her protective love for her family. But in the midst of my reflections, something strikes me. My forehead wrinkles. I can find a lot of books with animals, and a lot of books with white children, but I can't find any books on our shelves with characters who aren't white.

I shake my head, as if to disagree with myself. I was an African American studies minor in college because of my love for African American literature. We live at a school with students from over twenty different nations. We have friends from different ethnic and racial backgrounds than our own. We think of ourselves as people who care about seeing and listening to those who are different from us.

I want our kids to encounter all kinds of people in their daily lives and in the stories we read, but here I am giving our children a monolithic view of humanity, at least through our reading selection. According to this bookshelf, the world is monochromatic. Lions and mice are more likely to talk than children with brown skin are to have adventures and sorrows and dreams. I scan the shelves one more time—can they really hold no books that reflect diverse perspectives and experiences?

I've always believed that books can and should act as a

portal, a way to guide our imaginations, to build empathy and trust for people who don't look like us and don't live in similar settings. But here I am seeing my bookshelf not as a door but as a mirror, a mirror that shows me my white skin, my stable and traditional family, my remote and safe neighborhood, and little of the expansive world beyond.[1]

Where we live, local farms nearly outnumber local storefronts. Our town has no stoplight and no fast food. There are seven billion people in this world, but precious few cross our paths most days, and those who do reflect only this small corner of reality. A few steps out our back door, we can traipse down a trail that brings us into 2,500 acres of protected forest. We placed a bird feeder out the kitchen window this spring, and every morning William and I gaze outside. We share the exhilaration of spotting the shining blue wings of an indigo bunting, the bright yellow breast of the goldfinch, the stain of deep red on the throat of the grosbeak. Given how isolated we are from the world's diverse human populations, I had always intended for our books to provide a way into conversation and questions and even connection with people who share our loves and hopes and vision for the future, if not our particular situation.

We walk to the library later that week, and the kids revel in the beanbag chairs and computer games while I scan the shelves for titles that will expand our reading repertoire. I remember *Roll of Thunder, Hear My Cry* by Mildred Taylor from my own youth. The details come flooding back as I page through. Taylor won a Newbery Medal—the highest award for children's literature—for this story about the Logans, a landowning African American family in Mississippi. She paints a portrait of a complex web of generations struggling to retain their dignity and hold on to their hard-earned property in the midst of the Jim Crow South. But the plot hinges upon a group of white men who lynch three black men by setting them on fire. I place the book back on the shelves. I can't bring myself to introduce our kids to the history of the violence done to African Americans in the United States quite yet.

We walk home with a stack of picture books. Marilee squirms in her stroller. Penny and William stand next to each other as we wait to cross the street. Even though they are two years apart, with their light brown hair and similar size, people often mistake them for twins. Their bodies are different—William's wiry and strong, filled with compact energy. Penny still has a round belly, and she still tires even from activities like walking home from the library. She wears glasses, and braces on her ankles, and she has been smaller than her peers since birth. My role as their mother often seems reduced to keeping them safe. It feels irresponsible to expose them to horror just because I want to introduce them to a bigger world than our provincial existence. Or because I want to assuage my own guilt at living a life governed by concerns like whether to pay extra for the organic vegetables at the supermarket or how to handle the ant infestation in the kitchen. We return to *Charlie and the Chocolate Factory* that night.

The next day I call my friend Niro, whose parents both came to America from Sri Lanka. Niro is married to Ed, a surgeon whose family comes from Puerto Rico. They have four kids of similar ages to mine, and Niro is one of the few people I have known long enough and well enough that I don't worry about saying the wrong thing when the subject of race comes up. I know I might stumble over my words or betray my own ignorance or even say something unintentionally offensive, but Niro has always been gracious to me. Her ability to listen without judgment was evident when she lived in the room next door to me in boarding school, welcoming an unending flow of friends and younger students who poured out their troubles. Her gift of listening has led to her career as a therapist. Soon after we greet each other, I ask, "How do you choose books to read to your kids when it comes to race?"

Even though I can't see her, I can picture her—big brown eyes and curly black hair, offering me a compassionate gaze as she considers my question. She says, "You know, raising kids in a biracial home, the issue of race comes up almost every day. So reading is a place where we just let the kids pick the books they want. It's actually nice to have an area where we aren't talking about race all the time."

She explains further how her kids naturally gravitate toward book covers with images of diverse characters and how they don't read that many classics. But in our household, we rarely read contemporary fiction with our kids. Up until recently, I have always assumed that the books that have made it through the gauntlet of time comprise the highest-quality children's literature. Now, I am trying to find classic children's chapter books about people of color. Niro doesn't have any to recommend.

I hang up the phone and head back to the library, walking slowly along the crooked sidewalk in front of our house, past the town green and the Congregational church with its white clapboard siding. I assume my own ignorance has limited our bookshelves' scope, but I soon learn that children's books by and about people of color simply haven't existed in substantial numbers until quite recently. According to the Cooperative Children's Book Center at the University of Wisconsin, even as recently as 2013, only 94 of 3,200 books published for children prominently featured black characters.[2] I page through the records of Newbery Medal winners with a notepad in hand. If my rough calculations are correct, 8 percent of Newbery Medals have gone to books depicting the African American experience, even though the population of African Americans hovers around 13 percent. A similar disparity shows up for characters from other non-white racial and ethnic backgrounds. If I want to confront the problem of underrepresentation on our bookshelves, I have to confront a history of underrepresentation in the entire publishing industry. Which means I have to confront more than my own ignorance. I have to confront the subtle but pervasive power of whiteness.

In college, I read a collection of essays by novelist Toni Morrison called *Playing in the Dark*. It contains her reflections on the effects the presence of African Americans—what she calls "an American Africanism"[3]—has upon the plot, theme, and character development in classic American novels like *Uncle Tom's Cabin* and *Moby-Dick* and *The Adventures of Huckleberry Finn*. She suggests that white Americans—in literature as well as in the prevailing narratives of our nation's founding—understand the concepts of freedom and justice through contrast with their opposites. In subtle ways, American literature written by Americans of European ancestry has helped white Americans understand ourselves as pure and beautiful and good through the contrast with those of African ancestry, whom authors have often portrayed as dirty, ugly, evil, or dark. Morrison writes, "Africanism is the vehicle by which the American self knows itself as not enslaved, but free; not repulsive, but desirable; not helpless, but licensed and powerful; not history-less, but historical; not damned, but innocent; not a blind accident of evolution, but a progressive fulfillment of destiny."[4]

The cultural stories we tell about freedom and goodness and whiteness depend upon their opposite—blackness—and this theme shows up in the literature of Hemingway and Fitzgerald and Cather, literature that seems to have little to do with race. Perhaps Morrison would say that the historic absence of children's literature with black characters was an attempt—intentional or implicit—to keep white children "pure." I wonder, as I find myself rejecting books like *Roll of Thunder* and *Sounder*, the few chapter books I could unearth from decades ago with African American characters—am I appropriately limiting my children's exposure to hatred and suffering in the world? Or am I perpetuating a myth of white purity?

Every night at home we return to our reading ritual, that time of sweetness and serenity and friendship. But I start to see another dynamic at work in the books we read—the little Oompa Loompas in Willy Wonka's chocolate factory who resemble slaves who have been rescued (or captured?) from somewhere far south of England.[5] The Calormen in The Chronicles of Narnia with their swarthy beards and dark skin and evil presence.[6] The tension throughout the Little House series between Ma and Pa Ingalls and the Native Americans their white settlements displaced. Our kids are too young to understand these dynamics fully or to notice all these details. But I grow increasingly concerned that our reading is constructing for them a view of the world that places people with white skin and wealth and power at one end of a hierarchy and people with brown and black skin at the other. What if, in my attempt to bypass the injustices of the past, I am only underlining them, albeit in a subtler form?

I reach out again for help, this time with an email to my friend Patricia, an African American writer and teacher with children and grandchildren of her own. I explain my reading predicament and write,

> When did you introduce your kids to the horrors of slavery and Jim Crow?

She responds,

> I'll never forget my absolute shock at seeing Emmett Till's tortuously distorted face as he lay in his open casket, after his lynching in Mississippi, in a photo in *Jet* magazine. I was horrified and still young, but such horrific tragedies seemed to comprise our life, and nobody was shielding me from that. To not know about such things would've left me dangerously vulnerable, subject to making deadly mistakes—like the time I sort of walked towards a "whites only" drinking fountain in Durham, North Carolina (to get a drink of water?), and every adult in my family yanked me back from that forbidden water. I guess I'm saying that I never DIDN'T know that people can be horrible to each other. My own children learned that by being African American themselves and getting treated badly by white school children, in the same way that I also was treated badly. The saving grace, I guess, is that I also learned that people can be wonderful to each other. Kind people at church, school, and other places taught me that. But I didn't get a pass on knowing about evil. Nor did my children. In fact, until reading about your concerns about *Roll of Thunder*, I never imagined that some parents even have a choice whether to talk about it.

Patricia's words settle into my gut like a piece of lead. I feel stuck—dissatisfied with the "classic" reading options that had seemed ideal until I began asking questions, and still worried about traumatizing our children with stories of lynching and hatred. Eventually I discover the Coretta Scott King Award, given annually to "outstanding African American authors and illustrators of books for children and young adults."[7] From that list, I notice a series of novels by Mildred Taylor that narrate more stories about the Logan family, the main characters of *Roll of Thunder*. Taylor's understated prose portrays a history that haunts the present. The Logans struggle with rage toward white people, and they practice the hard work of forgiveness.

I readily add Taylor's books to our shelves. For William, who loves facts and history, I purchase National Book Award–winner Louise Erdrich's Birchbark books, a series that portrays the same time period as the Little House books, but from the perspective of the Native Americans. For Penny, who gravitates toward realistic social stories like *Ramona Quimby* or *Tales of a Fourth Grade Nothing*, I find the Ruby and the Booker Boys series, about an African American third grader and her family. For Marilee, I expand the picture books on our shelves to include books with African American history, multiracial families and neighborhoods, and African American girls who dance and sing and play.

As the children grow up, they start listening to the audiobook of *Little House on the Prairie* in the car. On the third or fourth time through, Marilee and William are sitting in the back seat of the car when Marilee asks, "Momma, are all Indians mean?"

I pause the recording. I've paid attention to the dynamics between white settlers and Native Americans in these books, and I hope our children can pick up on the tensions within the story. "What do you think?" I ask.

"No," Marilee says, with a little frown, as if she's trying to figure it out. "Because all people are nice."

"Well, all people have kindness in their hearts, and all people have meanness in their hearts. But why do you ask if the Indians are mean?"

"Because they seem mean in the book."

William interrupts, "Marilee, it's like there was one really big country with a lot of land but not a lot of powerful weapons. And another country wanted that land, and they had more powerful weapons. So the country with the powerful weapons won. And then the Indians had to leave even though they were there at the beginning." He pauses and looks satisfied with his grasp of history, but then his forehead wrinkles. "Mom, it's not fair if the government keeps making the Indians move. It seems really selfish."

I nod my head. "It was selfish, William."

I cannot defend the decision—by Pa Ingalls or anyone else, including our own distant relatives—to settle the East and then push west at the cost of the decimation of native peoples. I cannot pretend that these stories with characters we have grown to love portray a pure or unadulterated past. In fact, I am grateful that these stories give my children a way to wrestle with our history—the glory and the shame of it, the complicated, messy, ugly, selfish, and sometimes beautiful humanity of it all.

Later, we read another of Laura Ingalls Wilder's books,

The Long Winter, and I am struck by her description of the snow that terrorized them that season: "The little town was alone on the wide prairie. Town and prairie were lost in the wild storm which was neither earth nor sky, nothing but fierce winds and a blank whiteness. For the storm was white. In the night, long after the sun had gone and the last daylight could not possibly be there, the blizzard was whirling white."[8] I don't know if Wilder intended to make a statement about race with this passage, but the words speak to me as if she is reflecting on my situation. How easily whiteness blinds me.

As our kids grow up and enter elementary school, they begin to learn about civil rights, and they study geography and culture. We talk about race and disability and other religions when the topics come up at home, and yet their lives look similar in many ways to my own life as a child, growing up in a small southern town. I struggle with the nagging thought that I am perpetuating a cycle in which I keep our kids safe at the expense of growth. I revisit the books I read as a child, the town where I grew up, the schools I attended, and most of all, the nostalgia I feel for my childhood. I start to question my children's futures because I am questioning how accurately I understand my own past.

I want the books we read to be more than a mirror. I want them to be a doorway so that our kids can learn about other times and people and places. I want us to be able to acknowledge the truth and beauty in these stories while also naming the selfishness and injustice of our ancestors. I want these stories that invite us to wrestle with a complex past to help us write a different story for the future. I want to find a way out of blinding and incapacitating whiteness.

chapter three

THE GOOD OLD DAYS

When I was a little girl, sometimes it rained so hard and long that our backyard flooded. Our house sat a few feet above sea level, a block away from the inlets of the North Carolina coast. When the rains came, there was always a chance that water would overflow the drainpipes, spill across the roadways, and fill the bottom of the yard with enough water to reach our waists.

We had no fear. No thoughts of snakes or disease or objects dislodged by the current and menacing our bare bodies with their sharp edges. We knew the Sunday school story of the Flood as one of triumph and hope—animals, a rainbow, salvation. We didn't learn about the waters of judgment. We never considered the destruction that primordial storm had left in its wake.

Black plastic garbage cans bobbed through the yard. Our sandbox—a wooden square with no bottom—abandoned its mooring and began to float. We stripped down to our underwear to wade through the murky pool. My long, blonde hair stuck to my back in cords. My sister Kate grasped my hand. We ducked our heads and stepped into the sandbox, pirates sailing the high seas. With our bare feet gripping the ground, we maneuvered our ship over to the jungle gym, where the swings swayed on top of the water. We plundered the floating landscape for treasures—an empty soda bottle, a cardboard box, a beach ball.

After the splashing and shouting and adventure was over, we retreated inside to mugs of hot chocolate made with warm milk. Traces of mud speckled our bare legs. My mother wrapped towels around our shoulders, and our eyes stayed wide and bright.

Mine was a happy childhood.

It lined up with the ones I read about in books, with a brick house and a tree-lined sidewalk and married parents and a few trials and tribulations over friendship and lost kittens and the chicken pox. The dogwoods bloomed in the springtime, and the branches of the magnolia trees invited us to climb toward the heavens, and kids ran around the neighborhood and played for hours. My parents never yelled. They provided everything we needed. We took piano and ballet and felt proud and safe and independent as we walked by ourselves the two blocks to Main Street to buy donuts and pastries on Saturday mornings.

In retrospect, I can see the typical marks of upper-middle-class dysfunction, of human dysfunction—some parents who got divorced, some rumors of affairs, alcohol meted out in daily reasonable doses and then poured freely all weekend long. But deep pain and conflict were masked, at least from the children, and the surface of our lives looked lovely.

In our part of town, the houses were spacious, even grand. Wraparound porches, verandas, ten-foot ceilings, wide-planked wooden floors, pecan trees shading the backyards. Three houses down, the town green stretched from the historic brick courthouse to the water's edge, with cannons standing sentinel, markers of the wars once fought, invitations now for us to climb on their backs and pretend to take a ride.

We lived within walking distance of the local plantation. Across an old wooden bridge and a road through the woods, past fields of peanuts and soybeans, stood an imposing three-story white manor house. Past the house, cottages lined the dirt road, with clothes hanging out to dry. We sometimes drove down that road on our way to the country club. I stared out the window of our minivan from behind tinted glass. African American tenants sat in rocking chairs on the front porches. The air was hazy and thick with heat, like a shimmering wall between us.

There were four of us, all girls. Amy Julia, Kate, Brooks, and Elly—family names. I was the oldest, the serious one, the one who always had her nose in a book. I read for hours every day, mysteries and novels and biographies of Clara

Barton and Eleanor Roosevelt and Florence Nightingale, cheap paperbacks, old hardcover series shipped down by my grandmother, reading primers my mother had saved from her years as a grade-school teacher, the poetry of Shel Silverstein, the latest award-winning children's novels. Reading was the refrain of my childhood.

Caroline took care of us a few days each week. She was a short woman with light brown skin, a round face, and sparkling eyes. She wore a white dress and white shoes, like a nurse. Usually she covered her hair with a bandanna, but every so often she let her thick curls frame her face. Whenever I came upon her, she seemed to have her arms outstretched, welcoming me. She was full of praise—we had such good manners, we did so well in school, we had such nice singing voices.

Caroline wasn't the only person who worked for us. There was also Vera, who helped with cleaning while Kate and I were at school. And there was Samuel—his lean body and sinewy arms, his long, stern face that broke into a smile when we got home. He saw to the lawn and any odd jobs my mother needed. He whistled while he worked, and every so often he would swoop me onto his shoulders, and I would rest my chin on his head, taking in the scent of tobacco, cut grass, and sunlight.

Vera and Samuel and Caroline reinforced the stability offered by my parents, as did the rest of the neighborhood—the other families with young children, the old ladies who lived on our block. In the afternoon, I would make the rounds to Virginia Hayes, who kept ginger cookies on hand in case one of us came to visit; to Miss Betty Applebee, with her unmarried status built into her name, who invited me to come in and play her piano; and to Elizabeth Sumner, with her flower garden and her little fountain and her white hair swept up into a soft bun. I was always welcome. Always safe. Always listened to. Always loved.

Those were my good old days.

I look back on my childhood with fondness, with nostalgia, but also with a creeping uncertainty about how good it really was. Those years were marked by comfort, security, and stability. Life seemed simpler back then. We watched *Sesame Street* and *Mister Rogers' Neighborhood* after school. None of the mothers in our social sphere worked outside the home. They volunteered at church and gathered for knitting circles and chatted with each other on the town green while the kids played tag within earshot. For people like us, that world was easier. Homogeneity—by way of race and class and religion and experience—was comfortable.

I have replicated many aspects of my childhood for our own children. They take piano and the girls go to ballet class and we live in a small town with comfort and safety and the corresponding risk of never learning how to fail or how to handle conflict or how to respond to injustice in the world. For years, I saw only the benefits of this way of life. It wasn't until I began to consider the whiteness of our family bookshelf that I began to question the way whiteness functioned in my childhood. It was only then that I began to wonder how good and happy and beautiful my childhood really was.

It took me decades to see that the portrait of goodness I had created in my memory involved only a small portion of the population, and that it limited and constrained as much as, if not more than, it offered. It cut me off from complexity. It dictated the boundaries of my relationships. It cut me off from hardship—both the hardship of engaging human suffering and the more mundane hardship of discomfort or even deprivation. Beyond the ways my own life was limited by those boundaries, the goodness of my childhood was built upon the poverty of others. I was running around outside while my mother sat on the green and chatted with friends because Samuel and Vera and Caroline were cleaning and mowing the lawn for $2.50 an hour. That said, had my parents not employed local African Americans like these three, they would have effectively denied them the only work an unjust educational system had prepared them to do.

I loved Samuel and Vera and Caroline, but I never stopped to think what their lives might have been like if they had grown up in a different place or at a different time or with a different set of social expectations. Samuel's stories of the Great Depression fascinated me—with only eggs to feed their family, no salt, no butter, no milk—but I didn't stop to reflect on the sorrow that lay behind those memories until I was much older. I wondered about the equity of a world where Caroline lived in a tiny house on the outskirts of town while we lived in a big house in the center, but I couldn't see another way to live. I simply received the warm embrace, the gentle attention, the love they offered, the freedom they gave me to read and ride my bike and laugh and learn and grow.

Years after we had moved north and Caroline had retired, she called my father. She asked if he would send her some money so she could buy a pair of prescription glasses. He said, "Of course, but why?" She wanted to learn how to read, she said. She had stopped going to school when she was six because her mama hadn't thought it was safe.

At first I heard that story as beautiful, a testimony to Caroline's perseverance and creativity, to my father's generosity, to the years of trust and respect built up between them. But then it struck me, like a blow to my windpipe. How many years had that longing gone unfulfilled? And how many of those years were spent with me nearby, curled up in a chair with a book?

I want to insist that my childhood was good, and therefore that the values inherent within it are worth conserving and passing along to our own children, and yet I have started to wonder whether the effort to conserve is by its nature an effort to exclude. The words *conservative* and *conservation* share a root—to "keep with" or to "keep together." I consider the importance of conservation in general—museums, national parks, historic homes. Conservation can be a fight against decay, a fight to hold on to truth and beauty, an act of hope that generations to come can build upon what we have already learned, what we have designated and set apart to preserve, to revere, to remember. But conservation can just as easily perpetuate decay, preserve unjust systems, signal an unwillingness to change because change involves risk and loss, an unwillingness to admit and confront and seek to rectify the wrongs of the past. Conservation can signal fear or even negligence, a refusal to face the needs of the present moment because they seem too complicated, too big, or too likely to require sacrifice.

If I seek to conserve the safety and wonder of my childhood, am I insisting upon a system in which some people have far more than they need and others—hardworking, faithful others—have so little that life becomes a constant struggle to survive? I have replayed Caroline's question for my father about the reading glasses again and again, wondering whether it wasn't an act of trust and respect but of defeat, returning years later to a white man to ask for money to learn a skill that should have been offered to her decades before. If my childhood depended upon this imbalance, is it possible to label it "good"?

And when I allow that question, that confession, the admission that something wonderful to me was connected inextricably to the deprivation of someone I love, I no longer want to return to the past. My friend Sonja once told me that "the good old days" sounded like code for exclusion to her, an African American woman from Louisiana. Those words had always sounded like nostalgia for something beautiful until I started to view my childhood through a different lens.

There are two ways of seeing my childhood town—as a segregated backwater or as a bucolic landscape filled with flawed but generous people. There are two ways to see my parents—as a couple who ignored conflict and repressed emotion or as a source of love and grace and provision. There are two ways of seeing my heritage writ large as a white American—as those who have perpetrated years of unjust oppression of native peoples and African Americans and immigrants or as the founders of modern society with its celebration of liberty and justice for all. I have always thought I had to choose. If I am grateful for my town, my family, my history, then I must not critique it. And if I name the ugliness inside that history, I forfeit the right to be grateful. I am starting to believe that both must be true, that I can hate the injustice and name the goodness of my life, that I can recognize my parents' flaws and thank them for their gifts to me, that I can stand in the discomfort of the grief and gratitude of who I am as a child of privilege.

In Sunday school, I learned the story of the Flood in Genesis through a fun song about Noah and exotic animals. We colored pairs of lions and giraffes and elephants. We played with wooden figures of the ark and its inhabitants. We cut out rainbows, the sign of God's covenant after the waters receded, the sign of hope. When I later read Genesis as an adult, I realized the horror implicit within the story. The violence upon the earth was so great that God decided to reverse the initial act of creation. What had been created good had gone so bad and grieved God so deeply that God decided to wipe it out—the animals, the plants, the human beings. Only Noah, his family, and a select group of creatures rode out the storm. The rest of humanity and creation drowned.

When I understood the scope of the story of Noah's ark, it scared me, both because I did not want it to be true, and because I feared the truth it contained. I wanted to turn away from a world with such depths of evil. I wanted to turn away from a God with such capacity for destruction. I wanted to return to the children's song, the construction-paper animals, the caricatured, sanitized happiness. And when I look back on my childhood, I want to ignore the sorrow, the injustice, and the pain that I now can see beneath the beauty.

In the Bible, after the Flood, slowly, hope arrives. God acknowledges that the human heart will always bend toward evil, and then God promises never again to curse the ground or to destroy the living creatures. In a literal translation, God sets his "war bow" in the clouds. He lays down his weapon of destruction, and it becomes instead a rainbow.

That rainbow in the clouds comes not as the bright and cheery endnote of a happy-clappy religious message. The rainbow comes as a symbol of both power and vulnerability, of a God who hates violence and injustice and yet refuses to give up on human beings. The rainbow is a symbol of love, yes, but love that comes through sacrifice. When I look at the "good old days" of my childhood, I need to acknowledge the injustice alongside the goodness, to wrestle with the past rather than glorify it.

I want to return to the wonder of a flooded backyard. Instead, I return to the mournful story of a flooded creation and the tenuous promise of a bow of light stretched across the sky.

chapter four

A HISTORY OF CANCER

Looking out my office window, I see rolling hills and blue sky in the distance. In the foreground, my eye lingers on the trees beginning to bloom and a cluster of forsythia, exclamation points insisting that spring has arrived. All three children now go to school every day, and my life has settled into a predictable and balanced routine. I drop them off—William and Marilee at a Montessori school that draws from a handful of nearby towns, Penny at our local public elementary school. I come home to a cup of tea with honey and almond milk, clean the remnants of breakfast off the kitchen counter, start the dishwasher, and transfer the laundry to the dryer before I sit down at my desk.

Today's work begins with a social studies textbook from the 1980s. The cover is silver, with a photo of a white marble capitol building on front. The title reads *North Carolina: The*

Land and Its People. I flip through the soft pages of this book we used in fourth grade to learn about the history of the state where I spent the first ten years of my life. The book is filled with colorful charts demonstrating North Carolina's topography, biographical sketches of noteworthy residents, and photos of children and adults at the beach, in state parks, in classrooms and workplaces.

In fourth grade, social studies was my favorite subject. It felt like seeing the root system of a tree, all the sources of nourishment, the underground branches sprawling wider than the trunk itself. We took a field trip to Williamsburg, Virginia, that year. We learned about the pirate Blackbeard, who used the inlets of the Albemarle Sound, which lay a block away from our front door, as a hideout. We studied the Edenton Tea Party, when a group of women from our town had refused to drink tea years before the more famous boycott in Boston. We learned about farming and water and recreation in North Carolina. But I cannot remember learning anything about slavery or the Civil War or segregation or the civil rights movement. I have tracked down a copy of this book because I want to know what I learned when I was a child.

I scan all 350 pages, and then I cross-check my findings with the index. In the entire book, I uncover three references to slavery. The first: "Unlike the Europeans, most of the Africans did not choose to come to America. They were captured in Africa and brought to this country by European sea captains."[1] I remind myself that this was written for an audience of nine-year-olds and read on, trying to keep my judgments at bay. The next reference contains an explanation: "Planters had slaves because growing tobacco was a lot of work, and the fields were very large."[2] I think of the unwritten assumptions in this sentence, that slavery was inevitable, a matter of necessity, without moral implications or choices involved. I wonder how my fourth-grade classmates, many with fathers who were farmers, responded to this statement of fact. They knew growing tobacco was a lot of work. They knew the fields were very large. They also knew, even if they didn't think about it, that slavery was not the only way to grow this crop. And that's not to mention the assumption that farming tobacco was important enough to warrant forced labor.

A few pages later, I find one more veiled reference to an economy built for centuries upon human bondage: "Almost half of the blacks in North Carolina today live on the Coastal Plain. Do you think it might be because of where their African ancestors settled?"[3] I flinch at the dehumanizing language and at the question itself—at the author's implicit insistence that we see the past in a positive light. And I shudder at the chirpy tone, as if the enslavement of thousands of people were a fun fact.

My fourth-grade textbook profiles only one African American man—Charles C. Spaulding—who grew a multimillion dollar insurance company in North Carolina. After detailing his business accomplishments, the textbook shares something Spaulding wrote in 1948: "I shall always feel grateful that my ancestors were transplanted to North America."[4]

Settled. Transplanted. It is linguistic whitewashing—painting over the ugly truth of hundreds of thousands of human beings torn from their homes, dying in sordid conditions, and consigned to generations of forced labor. I think of the words the authors could have used. *Stolen. Abused. Enslaved. Murdered.* I wonder what I would have thought of my hometown if the textbook had stated the facts plainly.

When I was growing up in Edenton, African American people made up 50 percent of the population, and virtually all of their relatives had come to the region by force. Their history went largely unrecorded, and the brutality, injustice, and despair that marked their past went unrecognized. I put my textbook to the side. I am not surprised by the unwillingness to acknowledge the history of slavery. I expected as much. Still, as I look out my office window at the bright spring day, this reminder of how white Americans have tried to ignore slavery and its effects makes me feel as though gray clouds hang low, weighing down the horizon with rain that will last forever.

A few days later, I hear an interview with journalist Isabel Wilkerson, author of *The Warmth of Other Suns*, a history of the Great Migration of African Americans from the South to the North and the West throughout the course of the twentieth century.[5] Wilkerson likens history to going to the doctor for a physical. The physician's job is to prevent disease if possible, and to treat it when necessary. I think through her comparison. When I go to a new doctor, I fill out a form. I note that my mother and my grandmother had colon cancer, and my grandfather died young of heart disease. The doctor responds by suggesting I get a colonoscopy ten years earlier than the time recommended for the general population. If I lie or give incomplete information to the doctor, it may well result in illness or even in my death. But if I am honest about my family's medical history, it might prevent sickness altogether, just as acknowledging current health problems could lead to treatment or even to healing. Wilkerson's simple illustration helps me consider how my individual body is connected to a long line of men and women who went before me. Knowing, and naming, my family history of pain and disease is a necessary first step in detecting the same issues early on and in preventing that history from repeating itself.

Once I think through the illustration on a literal and personal level, I can envision what Wilkerson is claiming about our collective heritage, the stories passed from generation to generation about who we are as a culture. I am starting to understand why my friend Patricia cannot conceive of raising her children without letting them know about the violence of the past, and I am starting to consider how to convey the same information more fully to our own kids.

If I imagine my fourth-grade classroom as a doctor's office, I was taught that North Carolina had a history of health. Wilkerson's analogy makes the words of my textbook read like a two-pack-a-day smoker who admits to lighting up once or twice a long time ago. And then there were the placards throughout our town that commemorated noteworthy events and people from the past—the brass teapot on a pedestal on the town green honoring those rebellious women of tea party fame, the signs with information about various governors and legislators who grew up in Edenton and helped establish North Carolina as one of the first states of this new nation, the Civil War monument that recognized the men who fought and died. When I look back on it, I realize all these markers pointed to white women and men. There was nothing to recognize the history of slavery or its insidious legacy.

Edenton. Eden-town. It received its name in 1722 in honor of Governor Charles Eden, but it seemed fitting to think the name came from that garden in Genesis. Its history was imbued with romance, like the place itself—the pirates lurking in the coves, the graveyard shaded by centuries-old trees with headstones dating back to the 1600s, the fact that it had not burned during the Civil War, leaving many stately old homes intact. Each year brought four distinct seasons, but mostly we enjoyed long springs and falls and stayed inside our air-conditioned house or played at the country club pool in the summertime. I grew up close enough to rivers and swamps and family farms to hold a robin's egg in the palm of my hand and see a baby lamb just after he was born and bump across wooden bridges with old men fishing over the rail. The scent of magnolia and honeysuckle, the sight of cypress trees in a flat expanse of water, the sound of laughter, of the courthouse clock chiming at bedtime—I thought those traces of comfort and beauty all signaled health, wholeness.

I think back to a conversation from a few years earlier, when Peter was teaching at a boarding school and we lived in a dormitory with thirty high-school boys. One of the senior prefects who lived in the dorm, Davis, was headed to Yale—a champion rower, a student with honors and awards, a good friend and a leader among his peers. After graduation, I was remarking on Davis's many gifts to his mother, and soon enough we got to talking about summer plans. They were headed south for a bit, I learned, to visit his grandmother in Chowan County, North Carolina. "Oh my goodness!" I exclaimed, clasping her hands in mine. "I grew up in Chowan County, North Carolina! In Edenton! My parents moved there before I was born!"

She smiled and said, "We come from Edenton too."

I said, "How did your family end up there?"

She rubbed her lips together before she replied, "My family has been there for a very long time."

Davis was an African American student born of two African American parents. I should have known our history in this country was different. My cheeks burned from embarrassment that I hadn't thought about the distinctions in our past, and at the same time, my throat clenched with some combination of anger that our histories diverged so much and hope because here we were, living in the same house, with Davis headed to one of the nation's top universities in spite of a heritage of oppression. I cleared my throat. I didn't want Davis's mother to notice my response. She didn't need to comfort me about the past.

When I was in college, I took an Introduction to African American Studies class. One of our textbooks for the semester was a slave narrative, *Incidents in the Life of a Slave Girl* by Harriet Jacobs. As it happens, Jacobs was held as a captive in Edenton. She grew up in the same town as I did, knew the same landmarks, saw the same sunsets. Her narrative mentions the courthouse, the Chowan River, the plantation on the other side of the wooden bridge. It was easy to envision the town she described—the grid of streets, the shade of the pecan trees, the view from the water. And yet the monuments of grace and comfort to me were emblems of abuse to her. The courthouse grounds held the whipping post. The plantation house stood as a reminder of a world built upon the carnage of hundreds and thousands of human bodies, a shelter for powerful white men who preyed upon women like Harriet Jacobs. To avoid the advances of one of those men, she fled. For seven years she lived in an attic crawl space, nine feet long by seven feet wide, before she finally boarded a ship in the middle of the night and sailed toward freedom.

I learned nothing about Jacobs, or anyone else like her, when I was in fourth grade. Instead I read about Charles Spaulding, grateful that his ancestors had been transported to North Carolina.

I didn't learn that our state had a history of cancer.

I attended the only private school in the county, a school that drew students from five surrounding towns. Each grade held about forty children. It didn't cost much to attend. On the bus ride to school, we stopped to pick up one student who lived in the trailer park on the outskirts of town. Many of my classmates' fathers were farmers or worked at the paper mill. One of my best friends—Suellen Jones—invited me over to play one afternoon. I followed her on tiptoe into her parents' bedroom—a small, dark, corner room with bare wood floors and a metal-framed bed. She slipped her hand under the mattress and pulled out an envelope and flashed a wad of money at me. "What's that?" I whispered. My mouth dried up. I could feel my heart thumping. "It's my daddy's," she said. "I think he's selling drugs."

For Suellen's parents, paying any amount of money for school was a sacrifice. For mine, it was an easy decision. Education had always been a priority in our family. My great-grandfather had been the headmaster of a boarding school. My parents had both gone to private high schools and colleges. In Edenton, our school was seen as the best academic option, with smaller class sizes and "less violence" than the public school. Everyone who went to our church and lived in our neighborhood went there. There was nothing fancy about it. The building was constructed of cinder blocks and formed an L, with a long line of classrooms off a linoleum-tiled hallway in one direction and a covered cement walkway that led to the junior-high classrooms, cafeteria, and gym in the other. It was painted pale yellow, like the belly of a baby chick.

When I was older, a friend mentioned that our school had been started because of desegregation.

"What do you mean?" I asked.

"Private school is one way to keep white kids going to school all together," she said.

I had thought segregation ended in the 1960s, and I had never considered why no African American students sat beside us in our classrooms. But when I looked into it, I discovered that the school had been founded in 1968, thirteen years after the Supreme Court had voted to desegregate the nation's public schools with "all deliberate speed." In the state of North Carolina, those thirteen years had seen one commission after another "study" the "problem" of desegregation as the vast majority of schools themselves remained separated by race. By 1971, the North Carolina public schools had become fully integrated, and a decade after that, I was attending a private school with no African American students. Private "academies" like ours had sprung up all over the South, charging low tuitions that made them affordable for most of the white population and providing a way to avoid what was seen as the problem of integration.[6]

Segregation functioned as a caste system designed to instill a persistent and pervasive social message that African American people were inferior to their white peers. This message of inferiority came through a lack of funding for supplies and building upkeep as well as through the denial of access to the white schools. The Supreme Court diagnosed a sickness throughout the public-school system in the South when it demanded the end of segregation. Their intended antidote to the sickness was integration. Many white people instead responded by setting up private academies not bound by the rules of the state. Until families like ours were willing to acknowledge that the sickness had infected us, that we were a part of it, that we were passing it along to the next generation even if we didn't want to—any attempt at a cure was incomplete.

During our last year in North Carolina, I came down with strep throat. I managed to convince my mother to keep me home all week, giving me enough time to read *Gone with the Wind.* I had heard it was the longest book ever written, and I wanted to earn the badge of honor of having tackled it so young. The grandeur of Tara captivated me, the love stories, the sorrow of a noble and beautiful world changed, ruined forever. I pulled my knees close to my body in the big wingback chair in the den, and turned through hundreds of pages describing a bygone time. I suspect that had I read a book written from the perspective of an enslaved woman, I would have been similarly moved and concerned, similarly filled with a sense of righteous indignation on behalf of a people who had suffered loss and heartbreak. But my imagination was shaped instead by the story of Scarlett O'Hara. It was the fall of the Old South that moved me to tears.

That spring, I prepared to celebrate my tenth birthday. I invited all my friends to arrive in a costume from a different point in history. I decided to come from the antebellum era, as if I were a young lady living on a plantation. I had never heard of the Middle Passage. I had no concept of the brutal and daily reality of Jim Crow laws. I had no understanding that North Carolina's history included an illness that could prove fatal without serious intervention. I imagined the past as a peaceful time filled with corsets and men on horseback and fancy drawing rooms and suitors. I rented a gauzy floral dress with a hoop skirt and twirled around and around on our porch, dreaming of Tara.

chapter five

BANAL EVILS

One morning in the spring of 1986, Mom woke us up before dawn. We slipped on our sneakers and wrapped blankets around our shoulders as we climbed into the back seat of our Volvo station wagon. Mom drove slowly, with a mug of Folgers instant coffee in hand. Past the water and over the wooden bridge, out to the fields of the plantation, to the largest open space we could find.

Mom, Kate, and I lay down on the blankets and cozied up to one another. We were looking for Halley's Comet, a streak of light that wouldn't appear again in Mom's lifetime. As we lay there, she pointed out Orion, the Big Dipper. We found Cassiopeia, the Pleiades. We never saw the comet. I suppose it should have been a disappointment, but it wasn't.

We tiptoed into the night and gazed at the heavens. We lay down in a field of darkness to count the stars, to search for the light.

A few weeks later, I learned we were headed north for my father's job. We would leave behind our house, with its wrap-around porch and basement cisterns and fireplaces that had once heated every room. We would leave behind the people we loved—neighbors and friends and Samuel, Caroline, and Vera. We would leave behind the cats who showed up on the back porch every morning. We would leave behind an unimpeded view of the night sky.

The whole first year in Connecticut was a lesson in difference. I tamed my accent, made my words crisper, faster. Amy Julia became AJ. I dropped "ma'am" and "sir," eliminated "y'all" from my everyday speech. I took a train for the first time. My chest filled with anticipation whenever we drove around, especially at night—all the lights and traffic and people. Just one town away, there was a mall with a Chinese restaurant and a shop that sold only cookies and other stores with clothes and games and toys and anything anyone could ever want. In Edenton, the only fast food was a locally owned fried chicken spot. Now we had McDonald's, pizza that could be delivered to our front door, Baskin-Robbins, and Taco Bell. Everything felt fresh and fast and new.

It didn't take long for me to realize that the people in Connecticut saw it that way too. They saw themselves as smart and capable. When I showed up at our neighborhood public school for sixth grade—young, small, and carrying a thick southern drawl—the administration assumed I needed to be placed in remedial classes for math and reading. That assumption, alongside the gentle teasing about my accent and honest questions about my background from classmates, helped me see myself through their eyes: ignorant. I proved myself in the classroom readily enough, but the implication that I was a racist, or at least that I had lived in a community of racists until moving to the enlightened land of the North, was harder to shake.

It snuck into comments in social studies class, about how backward people in the South were with their shotguns and chewing tobacco, their tolerance of groups like the Ku Klux Klan, their social segregation. Once, a friend asked if we had lived on a plantation with black people who worked for us. No one used the word *racist*, but I knew the accusation for what it was, and I felt its sting. It stung all the more because there was truth to it. It came up when I wanted to pull out one of our going-away presents—little Confederate flags on wooden sticks—for the Memorial Day parade, and my mother flushed and said she didn't think that would be appropriate. Or when I thought back to our years living in North Carolina, like the time when I was watching a movie at home as a child, and the camera panned over dozens of faces of people sitting together in church. My eye landed on an incongruity. "Mom," I asked, "why is there a black man sitting in that church?" I had thought it was against the rules.

Again, Mom's face wore a look of surprise, but her voice

was calm when she said, "Churches should be places where everyone is welcome."

I could tell I had said something wrong, but I didn't understand. Plenty of people in Edenton were black, but I had never seen a black person near our church. I didn't ask about it again.

My parents never challenged the racial dynamics of my hometown out loud, but they did complicate it for me. My father's best friend from college was an African American man named Sky. They were a study in contrasts—Dad standing five foot five inches tall in his work boots, Sky living up to his name at six foot six. Sky worked for the Democratic party; Dad was a registered Republican. Dad's white skin was freckled and his hair sandy blond. Sky's skin was light brown, his hair black and wiry. But when it came to intellectual affinity and the capacity for friendship, they matched each other. Sky has been in my life as long as I can remember—sitting on our front-porch swing in Edenton wearing his Yale T-shirt and asking me about my favorite books, explaining politics once we had moved to Connecticut and he was working for the Dukakis campaign, dancing at my wedding, meeting our children and visiting our new house when he took his mother on a cross-country road trip to celebrate her ninety-ninth birthday. I grew up without thinking about my segregated school and church, but I also grew up with Sky as a role model.

Jan Bates was a model of hard work and intelligence too. When we lived in Edenton, Mom and Dad stopped hiring local white teenagers to babysit once they met Jan, a young African American woman working to pay for her books as a nursing-school student on a full scholarship. Jan came on vacation with us in the summer. Whenever I crept downstairs after bedtime, Jan was at the kitchen table, studying.

And Mom had once taken me to see Dr. Slade, after a series of white doctors had been unable to identify the cause of my persistent headaches. Dr. Slade was the only African American doctor in town, and his waiting room had been filled with African American patients. Sitting on the table in the exam room, I detailed my habits, the trip to the neurologist, my medications. Dr. Slade folded his arms across his chest and tapped his index finger against his elbow and nodded. "How much water do you drink?"

I wrinkled my forehead. "I don't like water," I said.

"Young lady, you need to drink more water. I drink eight glasses of water every day, and I haven't been sick in two decades." He turned to look at my mother and nodded again. "Have her drink more water."

Even at the time, I felt a nagging suspicion of my own symptoms—like they arose from boredom or a need for attention rather than any physiological problem. Dr. Slade was the only one to suggest that the headaches arose from something relatively benign. I disregarded his advice. The headaches continued for a time, and I took a little white pill every day at school with water from the hallway fountain. The pills eventually ran out, and we didn't renew the prescription. The headaches ran their course—unexplained pain with an unexplained resolution. What struck me most from that time was that Dr. Slade was smart and confident, and quite possibly the only doctor to offer an accurate diagnosis. Despite his competence, Mom was clearly breaking an unspoken rule by bringing me to see him.[1]

Mom and Dad never said anything explicit to counter the system of social segregation in our town, but their willingness to quietly break those social rules eventually helped me see the cracks in the edifice of racial separation. As much as I missed Edenton, now that we lived in Connecticut, I was beginning to understand why my new friends saw my hometown as racist. But the racism wasn't what they thought. It wasn't cross burnings and hooded robes. It wasn't violence or even, at least in my hearing, racial epithets. It wasn't the white supremacy of swastikas or vitriolic comments. The racism of my childhood looked benign. From my vantage point, it even looked reciprocal, as if everyone had agreed that this was the way it was meant to be. African American men and women who worked for white families usually filled seats of honor during funerals and weddings—right up front with the mother and father of the bride. Many white adults shook their heads with sincere admiration at the faith and the perseverance demonstrated by the people who came into their homes and cleaned and bathed and listened and prayed. Despite the segregation, despite the inequality, despite the many ways the town was harshly divided into white and black, the two groups were also inextricably bound up with one another in an intimate web of mutual, if imbalanced, support.

I read *To Kill a Mockingbird* for the first time that year we moved north. I recognized Atticus Finch, a small-town lawyer who protects an African American man from falling prey to a lynch mob. When Harper Lee's only other novel, *Go Set a Watchman*, was published in 2015, I wasn't surprised by Atticus Finch's explicit racism in this earlier version of his life. In the reviews I read of *Watchman*, people concluded that Atticus from *To Kill a Mockingbird* was fundamentally changed and different. But I thought it was entirely possible that Lee simply portrayed the same Atticus with different emphasis in the two novels. In *Watchman*, Scout, the narrator, is an adult. She comes home from New York City and can see her town's, her father's, racism for what it is. She focuses on that ugliness. In *Mockingbird*, Scout is a child, her father a hero. She focuses on that beauty. It seems entirely possible—even plausible—to me that Atticus Finch was a southern gentleman who wasn't looking for social equality, but who nevertheless wanted to protect the lives and the dignity of the African American men and women within his community.

Many decades after the scenes depicted in Lee's novels, I could still name adults I knew who mirrored Atticus's way of thinking. It was a vision of society that still depended upon a racial hierarchy but that also spurned hatred and violence, one that affirmed the inherent value of all people but expected those people to stay in their assigned social place. One of my mother's friends put the paternalism into words when we were back in Edenton for a visit. She said, "The blacks I know are some of the most amazing people. I'm just grateful God designed them to serve in so many beautiful ways." She had tears in her eyes. Her father was sick, dying, and his caregiver, Claudette, stayed by his side around the clock. I realized then that I had always chosen to see the love and not the racism when I looked at the relationships between black and white people in our town. I knew the assumption that all African American people were designed to serve white people was a lie that perpetuated injustice, perpetuated evil. With my mother's friend, I saw prejudice at work. But I also witnessed her love for Claudette. The words stuck in my throat as I tried to respond.

When my new friends in Connecticut accused white southerners of racism, they were right. But it felt more complicated than that. It wasn't only that the racism in our town didn't take the shape of mob violence or curses. It wasn't only that the separation was bound up with affection. It was also that the North had its own version of the divide. In my town in Connecticut, some students from other countries attended our public school, but not one student was an African American. No one in our neighborhood. No one shopping on Greenwich Avenue. No one taking the commuter train into Manhattan with my father. The only people I saw with brown skin in the late 1980s in Greenwich, Connecticut, were serving us from behind the counter at McDonald's.

Some of the differences between North and South came down to demographics. As my fourth-grade textbook had noted, African American women and men comprised 50 percent of the population of eastern North Carolina. The other 50 percent was white. In Connecticut, as with much of the nation, the state was majority white, and the white people clustered together in the suburbs. So the northerners talking about southern racism were naming something true, but they were doing it from a distance. My classmates were right to insist that African American people deserved equal treatment under the law and desegregated schools and social systems. But my new friends also ran the risk of caricaturing the white people in the South, losing their complexity, their capacity for both good and evil. What's more, in distancing themselves from the white people in the South, they failed to see their own legacy of complicity in a system of inequity.

When I was researching Edenton, I found a book detailing the history of the plantation near where I grew up. I paged through records from the days of slavery. As it happens, the plantation owner had ordered hats and socks and mittens from New Milford, Connecticut, a town fifteen minutes away from where I now live. Manufacturers from my region of Connecticut clothed the slaves, and they profited from it.[2] I hear reports on the radio about Aetna and Travelers—insurance companies in Hartford, Connecticut, companies where people in my family have invested and worked—companies that insured southern slaves so that owners could recoup their losses in the event that their "property" died. The Congregational church that sits down the street from our house has stood for centuries as an emblem of small-town New England life. In the 1840s, members of this community who opposed slavery had their church membership revoked due to their radical views. We have a history of racism in the North, too.

To this day, public schools in Connecticut are more polarized by race than those in North Carolina,[3] and the schools comprised predominantly of children of color spend less money per pupil and graduate fewer high-school seniors.[4] Here it is a racism of comfortable homogeneity, racism without relationships, racism without love, which threatens our communities just as much as the more overt systems of social segregation and oppression.

White people in the South have handled the problem of race badly. But that's not the same as saying that white people in the North have handled issues related to race any better. White people in the North just have been able to pretend that the problem didn't exist. My experience in two towns showed me that the disparities in education and economic opportunity between white and black Americans exist regardless of geography. Scapegoating the South or the cities perpetuates a state of convenient denial on the part of white suburban or rural dwellers like me.

Middle-school social studies classes didn't help me resolve the tension I felt when I wanted to defend some of the beauty and love of my experience living in the South while also acknowledging and despairing of the evils of racist systems there. But over the years, I found authors who helped me put words to my past—Harper Lee first, and later William

Faulkner, with his mournful novels that tap into the painful dance of intimacy and exclusion that rotted the core of relationships.

Besides Faulkner, I was introduced to Flannery O'Connor and her insistence on the full humanity—the depraved and wondrous humanity—of white and black southerners alike. In her stories, no one emerges as a hero. For O'Connor, everyone is in need of salvation, the educated white people most of all. In high school, I also began to read Toni Morrison, who writes with restrained prose about the horrors of slavery and its enduring brutal legacy. In Morrison's novel *Beloved*, one character escapes from slavery, and as she crosses the river that marks the transition from captivity to freedom, she feels her heart beating for the first time. With that simple image of an old woman who never knew the beating of her own heart because her heart had always belonged to a white master, I caught a glimpse of the pain, the centuries of pain, inflicted upon the African American population. I had never imagined how much slavery stole.

Scholar Hannah Arendt coined the phrase "the banality of evil"[5] to describe the way evil functions—not as overt horror but as small cowardly actions in keeping with the status quo. Arendt was writing about the Holocaust, but the racism of my hometown might count as yet another example of banal evil, evil that is all the more insidious when it masquerades as orderly relationships, evil that glosses over poverty and hopelessness with reassuring words of "just like family" and professions of love. But when I use the word "evil" to describe the ongoing racism that supported and engulfed my childhood, I feel myself pulling back. There was goodness present too.

I hesitate to claim that there was something beautiful in the relationship that existed between my family and Caroline and Vera and Samuel. Or that there was something good and true in the relationship between the Cuthberts, the Joneses, the Hubbards, the Wills, and the African American women and men who did their laundry and loved their children and blessed them at their weddings and cried at their funerals. I recognize the objective view that would say Caroline had no choice but to serve us with cheer, that her livelihood—as meager as it was—depended upon us. I recognize the complexity of claiming a relationship of love when such imbalances of power and education and social standing and opportunity are involved. For all I know, her affection was as prescribed as the white uniform she insisted upon wearing to work. And yet, when we visited Caroline's house, our pictures stood framed in her small and impeccably clean living room. Her husband thanked our family in her funeral program. I believe that Caroline loved us. I know we loved her.

I wrote the other family from Edenton whom Caroline worked for to see what they remember of her now that she has been gone for two decades. I learned that before she came into our lives, her only child, her son, had moved away from Edenton, married, and had four children. He later killed himself and his wife. Caroline wanted to take the kids, but she was poor and couldn't read and she was not able to gain custody. She rarely saw her grandchildren after that. She gave us her love instead. I had not known about Caroline's suffering. As a child, I didn't even know about the more general history of suffering among the many African American people in our town. I lived in happy ignorance.

In Edenton, the history of injustice was intertwined with a history of intimacy. The intimacy fooled us into thinking pain wasn't present, that evil wasn't really part of our culture, that suffering wasn't lurking beneath the love and tugging, with subtle persistence, threatening to pull us all under, black and white together.

chapter six

THE ROTATION OF THE EARTH

The alarm chimes early. Peter is away for work, and the children are asleep, but I force my eyes open as the flat white light of summer announces a new day. I pull on shorts and a T-shirt and head downstairs, iPhone in hand. I start an exercise video, mute the voice of the chirpy workout instructor, start running in place, and listen to NPR's *Morning Edition.*

Our family moved from New Jersey to Connecticut four years ago now. I have adjusted to the rhythms of this place—the lack of cell phone service and the half-hour drive to all the big-box stores. I have adjusted to the beauty here, beauty that asks for patience and then boasts every so often—the bloom of the daffodils in the spring, the stargazer lilies in their summer splendor, the red of the Japanese maple in autumn, the frosted trees that line our drive to school in the winter. I know the mailman and the children's librarians by name now. We hike these woods and take in the understated grace of our surroundings—the river, the rocky paths and gnarled roots, the canopy of trees. We have discovered the back road that offers a view of the lake at sunset with its purple sky and dancing light. When our children are all grown up, they will think back to this place as home, even if we have moved away by then—this big white wooden house with its black shutters and red front door, this quiet street, this view of hills and meadows.

The news I hear every morning as I exercise often feels dissonant. The news is flashy and quick in a way our town refuses to be, but it's more than that. The reporters tell stories that capture a tension between individuals and their local environments that we don't experience. Our town holds plenty of anger and sorrow, but the grief we know is personal, from a house fire or an uncle who overdosed on opioids or a mother with an Alzheimer's diagnosis. This morning, I listen to an update on the shooting of Philando Castile, an African American man who died at the hands of a policeman near Minneapolis after he was pulled over for a broken taillight. His girlfriend was in the passenger seat, her four-year-old daughter in back.

I finish my workout and bring my phone, and the voice of Steve Inskeep, with me into the kitchen. I pour three cups of orange juice and listen to the shouts of protestors over the airwaves. I fill three mini ceramic bowls with berries, and I hear a description of Castile's son, a teenager who will never see his father again. I reach into the refrigerator for milk, and I hear the recording of Diamond Reynolds, Castile's girlfriend, who narrates what happened after he was pulled over and, shortly thereafter, shot to death. My throat clenches as her voice rises in intensity, but I push away the emotion. My concern seems voyeuristic, as someone so far removed from her situation. As someone who turns off the radio when the children wander in.

Penny, eyes crusty, hands me her glasses. She leans her head against my rib cage in sleepy silence as I wipe the lenses clean. She swallows the tiny pill that regulates her metabolism and then removes the plastic back brace she has worn overnight to prevent her scoliosis from progressing. "I'm 'a go read," she says, scratching her head and shuffling toward the playroom. William's eyes look puffy most mornings, out of place on his lean face. He is nearly eight years old now and has cut his hair as short as it can be. I run my fingers over the stubble and give his shoulder a squeeze. Marilee starts the day with a hug. Her hair hangs straight and thick to the middle of her back. She wears glasses, like her big sister. The sharp edge of their blue frames presses into my belly as I pull her close.

After breakfast, the kids assemble their bags for camp. We check the list on the chalkboard: bathing suits, sneakers, tennis racquets, snacks, towels. Marilee cries when I spray sunscreen on her leg and it drips into her bug bite. Penny collapses onto the sofa when the thong of her silver flip-flop breaks. William crosses his arms and glares at me when I tell him to sit in the way back seat of the minivan. I am still thinking about Philando Castile and the little girl who watched him die, whose voice I heard on the recording as she offered comfort to her mother.

I often chase away fear when I think about our children—that Marilee will run across the street without looking, that I will chatter on with a friend at the beach and fail to notice Penny or William struggling in the water. Today my fear is brought up short by the recognition that I have never considered the way a policeman might see my son when he is all grown up. I have never worried that a stray bullet will pierce the wall of our home. Even the tragedies I imagine betray the privileges of my life.

For the past few years, the deaths of African American men and women at the hands of police have appeared regularly in magazines and in the news. I have memorized the names and stories without even trying: Michael Brown, shot in the streets of Ferguson, Missouri; Eric Garner, placed in a choke hold by police in Staten Island, New York; Freddie Gray, who died of spinal cord injuries after a ride in a police van; Sandra Bland, who died in jail after being pulled over for a traffic violation. The names go on, the stories similarly haunting, some about people who made mistakes, some about people who did everything right, but all about people who had no intention to harm the officers who killed them. I run through the list again, landing where they always do, with Tamir Rice, a twelve-year-old boy playing by himself in a park in the middle of the day. He was holding a toy gun. Someone in the park called 911 and explained that he saw a boy with a gun that was probably a fake but the police should check out the situation just in case. Tamir was fatally wounded by a white police officer within seconds of his arrival on the scene.

The frequency of these reports on national news makes it feel as if police tactics have suddenly escalated, as if racial profiling has reached new levels of injustice. But police interaction with black men has not increased in recent years. People like me—people who live in predominantly white America—have simply become more aware of it.[1]

I take a walk while the kids are at camp. Fluffy white clouds process across the blue dome overhead. William has told me recently that it isn't the wind that moves the clouds. What I see when I look up is the rotation of the earth. We are spinning so fast we can watch it with our own eyes, even if our feet seem to stand on immovable ground.

I pass the town green and the white wooden church with its Norman Rockwell simplicity. I cross the main road that cuts through town and pass a few more white wooden houses on my way to the graveyard, where headstones mark the lives that have inhabited this place for the past few centuries. I think again about how we ended up here. It seems natural now that we would arrive at a small Connecticut boarding school, given our heritage and the trajectory of Peter's career, but for years we had considered a different course.

We spent countless dinner conversations talking about a move away from whiteness, away from country clubs and catered dinner parties and classrooms with fifteen students discussing literature around large wooden tables. A group of Peter's closest friends from college had moved to a predominantly African American, low-income neighborhood in Richmond, Virginia, and we thought we might join them. Those friends—a multiracial group that included white men as well as men with families from Haiti, Sri Lanka, and India—had all been involved in efforts to acknowledge the historical racial divides within the church in America, and they wanted to participate in building bridges of reconciliation. They also had wanted to live near each other, and they had prayed for an inner-city community where people of color invited them into the neighborhood. Now, a decade later, two friends worked as doctors in the city, one served as a copastor of a multiethnic church, two taught school, one ran a nonprofit to connect kids in the neighborhood to the outdoors.

We took our family to Richmond to visit those friends one summer. Penny and William attended Vacation Bible School in the basement of a large Baptist church. They sang songs and made crafts and learned about Jesus. At the end of the week, we sat cross-legged amongst the other parents and watched a multicultural array of children, including our own, sing to us: "We are the light of the world. We are the city on a hill."

That week, four-year-old William asked questions like "Why does everyone here have brown skin?" and we explained that most people in the world have brown skin. He asked, “Why are all the cars parked on the street?” and Peter bemoaned the fact that our kids have such little knowledge of city living. The people in the neighborhood were friendly from the start—waving from their porches or nodding and smiling as we walked past—and we imagined what life would be like here. Our friends were honest about the challenges. They heard gunshots on occasion, and there were drug dealers in the area, and there were cultural barriers to overcome in getting to know their neighbors. Their presence was complicated—it contributed to gentrification, which forced some residents out of their homes when rents went up. And they could be accused of pushing the locals out of leadership positions as they became active in church and at school. But it seemed exciting to me, like they had found their purpose and were working to make a difference in the lives of the kids in their community, if no one else.

For us to join them was mostly a dream. The path from life as a teacher in a boarding school to life in a low-income urban neighborhood was not an obvious one. We had years of experience understanding the challenges of kids in affluent communities, and our exposure to students like the ones in this neighborhood was limited at best and inclined to be based on stereotype rather than reality. Still, we pursued the idea of a move. Eventually Peter discovered the existence of public boarding schools, schools built for kids who have trouble learning because of the difficult state of their home lives, whether due to homelessness or abuse or disruption in a family system. He visited the founders of some of these schools, and he began to apply for positions even though none of them were located in Richmond.

We were pulled toward these possibilities—first attracted to life in community with old friends, then excited by this discovery of urban boarding schools where we might be able to serve a different population of students than those we typically encountered. We also felt a sense of disappointment with traditional independent boarding schools. As Peter taught and coached students from backgrounds like our own, we started to wonder whether our lives were dedicated to helping the rich get richer. We wanted to inspire students to question their assumptions about what made life good, to look at the brokenness within affluence, to see their careers as vocations, paths forward because they were good in and of themselves, not because they were lucrative or prestigious. We wanted a change. Richmond, Brooklyn, New Haven, Boston. Peter traveled to schools up and down the East Coast.

I can envision it still: Instead of raising our children in the bucolic hills of Connecticut, sending them to private school, taking them out to dinner at our local pub where the menu includes a nightly salmon entrée, we would live in a simple brick row house. We would welcome neighborhood kids and host tutoring sessions in our family room. We would worship in a multicultural church. And then this book would write itself—a story of hope and redemption, for us and perhaps for the people around us as well, lives transformed through mutual sacrifice and growth.

But we did not choose this path.

I want to say this path has not chosen us. Those years of dreaming about a change were followed by job interviews and reading books about community development and watching television shows like *The Wire* and *Brick City* and praying and talking and thinking maybe we could do it. And then, at the same time that Peter inquired about job openings and received no response from any of the urban schools he had visited, he was offered the chance to attain a master's degree in history from Yale, paid for by his employer. The school would provide his salary and benefits while he spent a year away from teaching responsibilities. He would owe three years of teaching in return.

We found that social mobility is complicated in every direction. Just as social forces prevent individuals from breaking a cycle of poverty, people like us—born into wealth and whiteness, with expectations and opportunities for education and career advancement—forge relationships that connect us to more wealth and more possibilities within the world of privilege. Even though Peter and I often called our lives a story of "downward mobility"—he went from investment banking to teaching, I moved from nonprofit leadership with a decent salary to graduate school to writing and raising our kids—we remained tethered to our families and our networks. Peter didn't have a master's degree in education or the teaching certification or relationships needed to open doors for jobs in public schools. So we pursued the offer of the master's degree in history, and in so doing, we turned back to the world we knew, the world of privilege. We have made our home there.

We have made our home here, here in this neighborhood of white wooden buildings and black shutters and manicured lawns. I am walking through the historic part of town, with house after house set off from the sidewalk by its white picket fences and its stone walls. I run my fingers across the top of one fence line, this physical boundary that defines this lovely property, keeps children safe from the road, and signals where casual passersby should stop. I think about the ways in which privilege itself is a fence, a wall built over the course of generations, a wall that has surrounded us, protected us, cut us off, and kept others out. As an educated, married, Protestant white woman, I find myself stuck behind this wall of privilege. It feels safe, and comfortable, and there are plenty of everyday difficulties to occupy my attention. Still, the boundaries hem in my friendships and experiences and block others from the comfort and safety I enjoy. These walls have both protected me and cut me off—from risk, from growth, from acknowledging the hardships many other people face through no fault of their own, cut me off from connecting with people outside the fence through shared struggle or shared joy.

My ancestors helped erect this fortress of separation between WASPs and other racial and ethnic groups. The word "American" has often functioned as shorthand for people who look like me, people with a family history like mine, rather than as a national identity shared among all the citizens of this country, with liberty and justice for me and for Philando Castile and Tamir Rice and Michael Brown and their families. It feels safe and familiar within the confines of this wall, but I also imagine what it would be like for these stones to crumble. I wonder if there is any way for me to contribute to their dissolution.

When I think about social change, I am drawn to stories about women and men who single-handedly transform the lives of young people. I have enjoyed a dozen books and movies in which a teacher unexpectedly turns a classroom around. I have felt my heart thump with the thrill of civil servants who sacrifice themselves for the benefit of their city, of companies that create flexible work environments for parents or provide scholarships to children of employees. I stand in awe of our friends who have given up comfort and prestige in order to live in inner-city Richmond. But as much as white America (myself included) likes the narrative of white saviors, I am only too aware that white people do not have all the answers and our sometimes misguided desire to help others (and feel good about ourselves) can do harm in the process.

I think of the public example of Facebook CEO Mark Zuckerberg, whose one-hundred-million-dollar gift to improve the Newark public school system failed to achieve significant gains for the children in those schools.[2] Or I think of those same friends in Richmond, who regularly worry about the unintended negative consequences their presence has had in their neighborhood. Even with impeccable motives to help right the wrongs of systemic racism and historic injustice, moving outside this wall of privilege is not an easy solution, nor is it necessarily beneficial for the people ostensibly helped by the move.

So then I wonder if I should turn my attention away from those outside the wall to those within its confines. I'm aware of the social ills that plague my own community—the anxiety and depression and substance abuse. Moreover, I'm concerned about our seclusion. A racially stratified society harms not only the powerless but also the powerful. Any time we refuse to acknowledge the full humanity of another, we lose some of our own. But merely to shine a spotlight upon the sickness of white America is to become even more self-centered, as if justice should be courted for the sake of healing the wounds of whiteness.

The wall contains, protects, preserves, entraps.

I think back to Michael Ondaatje's 1992 novel *The English Patient*, where a disparate group of World War II refugees all find their way to the same villa. The staircase from one floor to the next has partially collapsed, and they use books to create steps. This makeshift staircase becomes an image of hope in the midst of the rubble of war, a suggestion that literature can rebuild civilization, that ideas and ideals can support progress, growth, and healing in a world that has been crippled, paralyzed, burned, and brought close to death. I think of that image and those stacks of books when I consider whether there is any way for me to participate meaningfully, truthfully, and helpfully in the current national conversation about race and justice, particularly as someone who was born behind the wall. Perhaps sharing our stories is a beginning.

I want to transform the landscape. I want to unwind the years of injustice—the lynchings and the laws of Jim Crow but also the desegregation orders that effectively fired thousands of black teachers, the banks that refused to lend money to most people of color throughout the past century, the slights and whispers, the turned shoulders, the quiet polite bigotry that closed doors and crushed dreams. I desire immediate change. But when I think through this type of transformation, I shrink back. What comes to mind are tsunamis and fires and earthquakes. Dramatic, instantaneous shifts that wreak tremendous loss and destruction along the way. I think of the images from the riots of the 1960s and beyond of cities ablaze, when injustice provoked outrage and then further destruction of the very communities already under siege. I am too risk averse to participate in or even to desire violent change.

And then I remember that ecosystems also change through slow, imperceptible crumbling and through slow, imperceptible accumulation of grains of sand. Salty seas have become deserts. Jagged mountain peaks have become rolling hills.

We need prophetic voices and actions—from Ezekiel and Isaiah to Martin Luther King Jr. and the Black Lives Matter movement. But we also need people who are willing to engage in quiet, persistent change. Together, landscapes can be changed so thoroughly they are no longer recognizable.

When I was born, 31 percent of African Americans lived in poverty.[3] By 2017, according to the US Census Bureau, that number had dropped to 22 percent.[4] The decrease is significant, but all I can see is a number that is far too high, a number that represents a level of vulnerability not known among the white population as a whole. White people enroll in and graduate from college at significantly higher rates than African American or Hispanic students.[5] Unemployment for African Americans is nearly double the rate for white Americans.[6] White people have nearly thirteen times the net worth of African Americans and ten times that of Hispanic adults. Even when controlling for factors like college degrees, white people get paid more than people of color.[7] Measurements that compare the present to the past show "progress" when it comes to racial justice, but even with progress, gross inequity remains.

And what about this educated white family who lives among the rolling hills of Litchfield County? In these years since I first noticed our white bookshelf, has anything changed, has anything progressed, for us? My examples seem paltry: We have visited the Martin Luther King Jr. memorial as a family. When Marilee asked, "What color skin does the Sugar Plum Fairy have?" I said, "She can have any color skin you want," and she said, "Then I will choose light brown." I received a Christmas card from Vera, who once worked for my parents, with a note, "Always remember: We are family." We provided a scholarship for one student to attend a private school in our friends' neighborhood in Richmond. We have invested in affordable housing there, as a way to make home ownership a reality for more families. Grains of sand.

Perhaps the reason knocking down the wall of privilege is so hard for me to envision is because it would require more sacrifice than I am willing to bear. Perhaps all I am willing to do is name the wall for what it is—a many-centuries-long creation that offers protection and opportunity while also cutting us off from the richness, diversity, and fullness of life. Still, I can hope—even with the tenuous offering of these words—to participate both in the work of eroding the wall and of building something new.

I finish my walk in our local nature preserve, a small mountain set next to a river. As I turn to head home, I pass a wall from an earlier era, when a house built upon a foundation of stone stood in these woods. The stones have crumbled, and the grass and trees have begun to erase them from the landscape. The walls of this house no longer prevent entry. They no longer protect any occupants. They have become a curiosity, an invitation to imagine a past we no longer inhabit.

chapter seven

INSIDIOUS IRONY

I am sitting cross-legged with my eyes closed. My hands rest one atop the other, facing my heart. I breathe in through my nose, slowly and calmly. I pray as I inhale, asking God to bring peace into this day, into my body, my mind, and my spirit. I then exhale slowly and calmly, trying to match in duration the two sides of the breath. As the carbon dioxide leaves my body, I pray that God would take all my worry, all my fear, all my stress. I breathe in God's peace. I lay upon God my anxiety. An uneven, cleansing exchange.

It started because I was drinking too much wine. One glass each night turned into two or three during the year we moved to Connecticut. On the weekends, at parties, it became three or four. Everything in my life was stable enough—happy kids, happy marriage, good friends, finances in good order—but my wine consumption increased increment by increment until I couldn't remember, or imagine, a night without it. I wanted things to be different.

I read a book about habits, and the author suggested observing the habit you want to change.[1] My observations helped me realize I drank wine for two different reasons—for peace and for pleasure. I wasn't too concerned about the times I drank for pleasure, but I got in trouble when I turned to wine for peace. I poured a glass on Monday evenings, when the thought of pushing through homework and dinner and bedtime and returning to the to-do list just felt like too much. I poured two or three glasses at cocktail parties when I was supposed to be a proper hostess but I would rather have been reading a book in bed. I poured a glass when I was alone with the kids and Peter was traveling, or when I was worried I wouldn't get an article written on time, or when I found out Penny had scoliosis and would need to wear a back brace for eighteen hours a day or that William was getting stomachaches at school whenever I was away or that Marilee was sad because her friend was moving. Whenever an occasion to worry arose, without even naming the concern, sometimes without even knowing I was worried, I turned to Chardonnay.

After making these observations, the habit book suggested replacing the old habit with something new. My yoga teacher offered the idea of turning my focus away from the wine and on to my breathing. So here I am, starting the day with a signal to my body and soul that peace comes from God, not from wine.

This pattern of dealing with anxiety through self-destruction began back in high school. Up until that point, I had been like a baby bird hopping safely and happily along a path of privilege. When I was thirteen, I graduated from my public middle school and moved to a private boarding school an hour away from our home. I had always assumed I would go to boarding school, like my mother and father, my grandmother and grandfather, before me. Once I arrived, I soaked in the benefits: small classrooms, continuous access to teachers, students from around the globe and from a wider array of cultures than in any other school I had ever attended, opportunities to try sports and drama and all sorts of club activities, to write for the school newspaper, to sing a cappella. In my class of one hundred students, my friends included Natalie and Jen and Audrey and Susan—other white kids with backgrounds similar to mine—but also Adi, whose parents had arrived from India; Chris, who grew up in Harlem; and my lifelong friend Niro, whose family introduced me to saris and Sri Lankan food and a culture of hospitality I had never witnessed before. Regardless of our towns and countries of origin, we shared the experience of living away from home, of eating institutional food, of regulating our activities and study habits and emotions without parents around. We shared the excitement of semi-independent living, and we shared the pressure of a school designed to prepare us for the rigors of top-tier colleges.

Barry Switzer, former coach of the Dallas Cowboys, once quipped that, "Some people are born on third base and go through life thinking they hit a triple."[2] Most of us at boarding school had been born on third base, whether we knew it or not. But clearing home plate still felt like a lot of hard work. Some of that work happened in the classroom—I studied for hours every night, reading novels and writing essays and conjugating verbs and working out geometry proofs. I received the rewards that accompanied hard work: learning that shaped and enlarged my understanding of the world, not to mention good grades and a clear path to college. Then there was the work of finding my place in the midst of a gaggle of girls who all lived together—a select group inclined to put pressure on ourselves to perform, achieve, and conform to every standard set for us by our culture. We played by the rules—in my group of friends we didn't drink, smoke, or do drugs, didn't hook up with boys, didn't sneak out of our rooms during study hall. We respected our teachers, took on leadership positions to serve as role models for younger students, and turned in our assignments on time. And most of us, like many of our affluent and achievement-oriented peers, were miserable.

By the winter of my sophomore year, I had a lead role in the school play, the top grade point average in our class, and a set of close friends. I also started involuntarily vomiting my food after every meal. I lost 15 of my 102 pounds over the course of two months. My mother took me to one doctor after another until we traveled to Yale New Haven Hospital to see a specialist. I sat on the examination table while a nurse checked my vital signs. She placed a blood pressure cuff around my arm and pushed a button so a machine could record it. It beeped to demonstrate an error. She tried again. And again. Even when she tried to find a reading manually, she couldn't come up with a number. She gave up and asked me to provide a urine sample. I walked back from the bathroom with an empty cup in my hand. The world had become opaque. As if through water, I heard a doctor talking with my mother about immediate hospitalization.

For the first few days on the pediatric ward, I lay in bed, an IV dripping a mixture of fats and sugars into my slender veins. On the fourth day, my mother says she knew I would recover because I asked her to bring me a book. I stayed in the hospital a full week as the doctors concluded from the pictures of my stomach—a gray wall of immobile tissue—that it was paralyzed. The food I ate simply sat there, without digesting.

They never determined a cause, but I have my own theories about why a seemingly happy, successful, fourteen-year-old girl collapsed that winter. I assume the pressure I had placed on myself, the pressure I had internalized from teachers and coaches and friends, overwhelmed my system so much that it simply ceased to function. My body offered a silent scream of protest, even if I couldn't bring myself to acknowledge it.

There was also the influence of my family. When we moved to Connecticut, I was ten years old. My father started taking the train to work in Manhattan every day, usually before I made it downstairs in the morning. He got home after the kids had eaten dinner, weary from the commute, barely mustering the energy to say hello. He woke up before dawn every morning to run for miles, and on the weekends he ran morning and afternoon, four long runs in total if time allowed. I hardly noticed his absence, or his sadness, but perhaps I felt it in my gut. Or perhaps I internalized a stoic approach to all adversity from my mother's side of the family. I come from hearty New England stock, from generation after generation of long, cold winters and making do, from a mother who only showed emotion during sappy commercials and a grandmother who thought hard work and a positive attitude could overcome every challenge. I come from a long line of thrift, in which things like body lotion and new clothes were seen as self-indulgent. Perhaps I needed to give myself permission to be needy. Perhaps I just needed to cry, and I knew it wasn't allowed.

Whatever the reason, my stomach was paralyzed, and I was sick. I fainted regularly when I moved from lying down to standing up. I refused to use a feeding tube and spent my days sipping one ounce every five minutes of a liquid nutritional supplement designed for elderly patients, because I couldn't stomach any solid food. I completed the spring term from home. I returned to school the following fall. I signed up for a full slate of Advanced Placement courses, sang in the auditioned choir and a cappella group, became the editor-in-chief of the school newspaper, and was selected as one of ten "monitors" to live with younger students. When people asked me about my illness, I said, "My weight is stable, but I still throw up occasionally." Occasionally. As in, every meal. I never forced myself to vomit. It still happened naturally. But I lied to everyone about the frequency because I wasn't interested in getting better. I called it an illness, and I could hide behind the reality of my physical condition. But my thinking bore all the hallmarks of a girl with a severe eating disorder, albeit a girl so tethered to performance and achievement she knew that, just like expressing strong emotions, eating disorders were not allowed. An illness, on the other hand, was not in my control. Illness didn't break the rules.

Many of my peers shared my obsession with the scale. Only a few others ended up in the hospital, but most of us lived with constant attention to fat and calories. And most of us continued to get good grades, hold leadership positions, and eventually, get into the colleges of our choice. We received admission to Princeton, Duke, Mount Holyoke, Middlebury, Dartmouth, Columbia. The privilege of an elite education gave us a foundation that other kids our age didn't have. But once that foundation was handed to us, it was our job to build and build and build. Privilege rewarded us, but it also demanded our obedience.

Twenty years later, I can look back on all of us with compassion. I look back, and I wish I had learned how to take risks and not just how to perform according to expectations. I look back and wish I had rebelled outwardly rather than internalizing all the pent-up angst over the growth and change of adolescence. I wish I had asked for help. I wish I had admitted that my paralyzed stomach was more than a quirk of my biology. I wish it hadn't been six years of bingeing and purging and shame.

And although my experience offers an extreme—both in terms of the extreme privilege of the boarding school environment and the extreme limits of a physiological and psychological illness that brought me near death—that extremity can also provide clarity on the problems, or at least the pressures, of privilege.

Now that I'm an adult, I no longer am working to increase my GPA or lengthen my college brag sheet, but the pervasive insistence on achievement and appearance remains. I begin my new morning breathing routine—praying for peace as I inhale, exhaling anxiety, looking for change in my drinking patterns—and around the same time William brings home from his third-grade classroom a poster of "fundamental human needs," the different aspects of human development that constitute a whole and healthy self. His colored-pencil sketches include a circle for basic material needs such as food (pizza), water, and shelter (a bed with a *Star Wars* blanket on top). For children like my son, these needs are met implicitly, by virtue of affluence. Similarly, when I was a kid, I never had to wonder whether food would be put on the table. Even though my parents required me to work and save for things like summer camp or a new computer, I never worried about whether money would be available in a crisis.

The next circle on William's chart includes psychological needs for relationships with family and friends. As I smile at

William's stick figure drawings of his sisters and classmates, I wonder whether our psychological needs have been met or stymied as a result of affluence. On the one hand, affluence seems to make relationships easier. In my case, it provides time, with money to pay for household work to be done by others, with money enough for me to work only part time and be at home after school, welcoming our children and their friends under our roof. And yet, our affluence also fences us off from other people. We can afford to pay for the "best" of everything—ballet classes and private swimming lessons and sleepaway camp and private school—and in so doing, we don't interact much with people who can't afford those opportunities. Unless we consciously choose for it not to, affluence cordons us into relationships with other people with wealth. It is easy for us to stay on the surface of our lives with these friends. We can pay for help instead of depending upon one another for it.

I'm curious enough about the relationship between affluence and well-being that I read a long report in *Child Development*. The researchers articulate my unformed thoughts:

> Affluent individuals are amply able to purchase various services such as psychotherapy for depression, medical care for physical illness, and professional caregivers for children, and in not having to rely on friends for such assistance, they rarely obtain direct "proof" of others' authentic concern. In essence, therefore, the rich are the least likely to experience the security of deep social connectedness that is

> routinely enjoyed by people in communities where mutual dependence is often unavoidable.[3]

It is as if those of us with wealth try to deny something core to who we are as human beings. Whether we like it or not, we are needy, and no amount of money will ever change this fact. When we try to outsource our neediness, we strip ourselves of the gift of relationships built on trust and hardship and care for one another. Perhaps it is that unwillingness to admit and face our human neediness that leads to a sense of deprivation among the affluent. Perhaps it is that unwillingness that leads to my third glass of wine.

William's chart from school goes beyond the material and psychological. The third circle contains spiritual needs. Here, too, I look at the data, and people with wealth present as needy. On a global level, the poorer people are, the more likely they are to say that religion plays an important role in their daily life.[4] According to a Pew Research Study in 2016, self-described atheists and agnostics are far more likely to be wealthy (defined as making $100,000 per year or more) than most Christians.[5] In my own life, a deep sense of spiritual purpose was missing from my adolescence. Growing up, my family went to church, and I believed in God in some abstract way, but that theoretical belief didn't ground or center my life before I got sick. Even once I could see my own helplessness, I still bowed to the god of achievement. I kept striving to repay a debt to the god of privilege, who had blessed me. And like all false gods, privilege turned out not only to be worthless but also to be bent on my destruction.

Privilege provides for material needs, but it seems to work against the fulfillment of other human needs. Instead, privilege correlates with some of the shadows of the human experience—eating disorders and anxiety and substance abuse, among others. As I consider these dynamics, I pick up a book that has been sitting on my bedside table for months, Madeline Levine's *The Price of Privilege*. I find myself underlining whole paragraphs and placing stars and check marks in the margins. After decades as a therapist, Levine saw her affluent clientele becoming more and more lost. She did some research, and she discovered that her anecdotal experiences of angst-ridden and apathetic teenagers could be documented on a broader scale. Levine looked at adolescents from affluent homes across the United States, and she discovered high rates of depression and anxiety. She also revealed a higher sense of disconnection from parents among affluent kids than among children living in poverty. Levine diagnoses the problem as a problem of materialism, a value system based on things rather than on relationships and character development. She, too, identifies privilege as a barrier to fulfilling human psychological and spiritual needs. She writes that many parents are "consistently making it to their [child's] soccer game while inconsistently making it to the dinner table,"[6] therefore communicating that children are more valuable for what they do than for who they are.

Levine's research squares with what I had experienced in

high school and with what I experience personally and with friends and family living in wealthy, college-educated communities. Gallup polls support this research, demonstrating higher rates of alcohol use among wealthy and well-educated adults than among lower-income groups.[7] The *Journal of Studies on Alcohol and Drugs* reports a higher use of both alcohol and marijuana among young adults who grew up in higher socioeconomic brackets.[8] Suburban teenage girls have a rate of clinical depression triple that of the norm, and affluent youth demonstrate high rates of anxiety and depression overall.[9]

As true and helpful as Levine's diagnosis of both the problem and its causes may be, what strikes me about my own situation and about the related rates of anxiety, depression, and substance abuse among both children and adults of privilege is the way in which the privilege of affluence allows us, and perhaps even encourages us, to focus on ourselves. The years of my illness were the saddest years of my life. But no one died. No one injured me with words or actions. I had a supportive and loving family, friends, and boyfriend. I got good grades, attended the schools of my choice and my dreams, enjoyed learning and leadership. I also weighed myself every day, worked out religiously, and exulted in the gaunt features that stared back at me from the mirror. I thought about myself all the time, which cut me off from relationships with others and from the energy and self-possession to care for others. I felt hopeless and helpless. Twenty years and three children later, I found myself in a similar place as a mother who drank too much every night.

The insidious irony is that in insulating us from the wounds of the world, privilege can make us become focused upon the wounds of our psyches and neglect the needs of our souls. Privilege allowed me to turn inward. I stayed focused on myself, and I stayed miserable. When I look at the data about depression, anxiety, substance abuse, and isolation among the affluent youth and adults today, it seems I'm not alone. Wealth does bring happiness up to a point. We need basic material security. But people with no worries about their material needs have the luxury of becoming self-centered, which often means becoming self-destructive.

Back in high school, when I became so ill that I entered the hospital and my whole future was in jeopardy, I found myself asking spiritual questions for the first time. If the God I had heard about in church was actually real and good and loving and powerful and cared about me, then I needed that God in a way I had never needed help before. I started asking questions and reading religious books and reading the Bible and praying tentative prayers. And I began to believe that God had been ready and waiting for me, loving me in the midst of my helplessness all along.

There's a passage in the Bible where Jesus talks about the reasons humans worry. He explains that without God, it makes perfect sense to be worried about what we eat and what we wear. Without God, we should run around frantically providing for ourselves. But as it turns out, Jesus says, you don't need to worry. God loves you and will take care of you. For Jesus' original audience, the worry was directed toward material needs, but I imagine Jesus speaking into our context, saying, *You don't need to worry about social status. You don't need to bow down to the god of career success. You don't need to become an expert parent.* Rather, says Jesus, "Seek [God's] kingdom, and these things will be given to you as well."[10] The language is a bit obscure, but I think he means that because we can trust God with our lives, we can be free from worry. God will provide what we need—materially and psychologically and spiritually—so we don't need to seek after those things directly. Trusting God to meet our needs frees us up to focus on God's Kingdom instead. Jesus invites us to set our hopes and focus our energy upon the goodness of God breaking into our world. He invites us to look for and welcome love and justice and peace and joy.

I used to think that privilege provided a foundation for personal growth and for discovering a purpose bigger than me because it took care of my material needs. But time and again I have found that the provisions of affluence suck me into a web of self-centeredness where I focus on myself, my own resentments and disappointments, and I get stuck in anxiety or an eating disorder or drinking too much all over again. Privilege does provide more than enough to take care of my material wants. But we human beings need more than stuff. We need friendships. We need relationships based upon mutual vulnerability and trust. We need spiritual lives that not only fill our souls but also give us a sense of purpose beyond ourselves, that extend an invitation to participate in bringing light into the world.

I thought that having our material needs satisfied would mean freedom from worry, but it only provided freedom to worry about other things. I thought it might free up privileged people to satisfy their psychological and spiritual needs, but the data and my experience don't bear out my assumptions. William's chart of human needs originated with Abraham Maslow, who envisioned those needs as a pyramid or hierarchy, with material needs as the foundation that supports all the others.[11] Perhaps this hierarchy of needs is upside down. Perhaps if we all paid attention to our spiritual needs—the need for meaning, the need for forgiveness, the need for love—the material needs would be met, not least because the people with the most money would start caring less about holding on to it and consider what it might mean to share it more widely. All the money in the world couldn't change the anxiety I felt as a teenager trying to achieve my way through school. And all the Chardonnay in the world couldn't bring me the peace I sought night after night when our kids were younger. But admitting my needs and receiving the mysterious love of God could change me.

I breathe in peace. I breathe out anxiety. An uneven, cleansing routine.

privilege walk

I am a few weeks into my sophomore year at Princeton. I think I am showing up for a presentation about race, class, and gender. But the chairs have been pushed to the side of the meeting room in the Community and Religious Life building. Clustered together with my peers, I listen to a few words of welcome, and then the student organizers ask us to line up side by side across the middle of the room.

We number around sixty, and we stand close enough to hold hands. I find myself in between another white woman and a lanky black man named Michael. I catch his eye and offer a quick smile. He and I share a discussion section for our Introduction to African American Studies class. Michael is one of the few people I recognize. None of my close friends are here.

One of the student organizers balances on a plastic chair, commanding attention by the precarious nature of his stance. He welcomes us again, then instructs, "If your ancestors came to the United States by force, take one step back." Michael eases away from me. I stay put.

"If there were more than fifty books in your house growing up, take one step forward." I take a step.

"If you were ever stopped or questioned by the police because of your race, take one step back." I think of the time my boyfriend and I had decided to avoid his mother's oversight and make out in a car. A policeman had rapped on the window, telling us—firmly but politely—to move along. I glance over my shoulder. Michael steps back again. He stares straight ahead.

The O. J. Simpson murder trial has been in the news

lately. We don't talk about it much on campus, but the only people I know who think O. J. should be presumed innocent hail from my African American studies class. It is in class that I first hear the term "Driving While Black." I have learned that many of my classmates feel the color of their skin is as incriminating as a bottle of alcohol behind the wheel. "Driving While Young, White, and Freckled" doesn't bring with it the same concerns.

"If you have ever felt uncomfortable about a joke directed at your gender, take one step back." The girl next to me grimaces and moves. I scroll through my memory. I have heard blond jokes before, but I can't honestly say they made me feel uncomfortable. Annoyed, sure. But confident that they didn't apply to me.

The list continues:

If you were embarrassed about your clothes or house while growing up, take one step back.

If your parents or guardians attended college, take one step forward.

If you were raised in an area with crime and drug activity, take one step back.

If you have ever traveled outside the United States, take one step forward.

If you were raised in a single-parent household, take one step back.

With every potential step back, the line of people nearby fades. With every step forward, I feel my heart thump a little harder. Family vacations, private school, a person who cleaned the house, summer camp, museum visits, days off for religious holidays, discretionary money—each one a step forward. Each one creating distance.

Over the course of the time, I take two steps back—one in reference to degrading statements about women on television, one about the gaze of men at construction sites. But as a white, heterosexual, educated, Anglo-Saxon Protestant young woman who grew up with a stay-at-home mom and a dad who worked in finance in Manhattan, mine is among a handful of similarly privileged lives. All of us who advance to the front of the room have white skin.

When we gather in small groups to discuss the exercise, one girl looks at her fingernails as she talks. "It felt pretty hopeless to keep taking steps back."

Michael nods. "Hopeless and infuriating," he says. "Like, I worked hard to be here, and I'm still at the back of the room." A murmur of assent travels like a spark around the circle.

I am surprised by these comments. I thought they might feel the opposite—amazed by their accomplishments in spite of the odds, bewildered by how successful and poised and gracious they are as students at an elite university even with this legacy of oppression. But this activity was not designed to demonstrate strength in the face of adversity. It was designed to demonstrate the unwitting advantages of privilege. It was designed for people like me.

Even though we sit next to each other, I feel as though I am still standing at the front of the room, alone. Protests run through my mind: *Is it my fault that I ended up in front? I didn't mean to be there. I'm sorry.* But I remain silent.

What is there for me to say?

chapter eight

BLESSED

Told one way, it is a miracle that I met my husband. Told another, it was the inevitable product of social forces. My whole life is a story that represents the loving and purposeful hand of God or the hand of affluent white America. Or maybe it is both.

We met when I was a senior in high school. By then, I had given up on the thought of having a boyfriend. I had been "the sick girl" for a long time, and then I had a religious awakening that turned me into what the rest of campus dubbed the "class Bible-beater." For the record, I never forced a Bible on anyone, but I did experience a rather radical encounter with the divine the summer after my illness began.

My parents were churchgoers, and I had dutifully progressed through confirmation classes and worn a white robe and stood before the congregation and assented to propositions about Jesus and God and sin and all the rest when I was in middle school. But before my illness, God was exactly that: an interesting proposition, not a source of help or comfort or care. I wanted everything I had said in church to be true, but I wasn't convinced. When I got sick, I started to pray, little whispers of longing. One of my church friends invited me to go with her to a Christian camp, and I said yes. I heard talks about the same topics that had been offered in Sunday school and youth group, but they mattered more now. If I was at my core a broken human being in need of the love of a good and everlasting Creator, then maybe there was hope for me. Maybe I could get well.

I still wasn't certain about God's existence or God's goodness, but I knew something needed to change in my life. So I decided to pretend that God was real and personal and listening to me. I sat on the shore of a lake and I prayed about whether I should return to boarding school or stay home and go to public school. I felt pretty sure public school was the answer. It held the comforts and protections of family and friends and church. Less pressure. Fewer comparisons. But when I was praying, I heard what was both an external voice and a voice that came from deep within me, and the voice said, "Go back to boarding school, and take me with you." That voice tipped me into faith—into confident and lasting belief in God's presence and God's care. It also tipped me back to boarding school, where I arrived the following September with a literal cross in my pocket and a desire to let everyone else know about this God who had changed my life. As one friend put it, warily, I had *got religion.*

I've had many experiences of what I would call divine direction over the years—times when I was praying about a situation and it resolved in an apparently miraculous way, times when a passage from the Bible seemed to be written for me right here and right now even though the words had been penned thousands of years earlier, times when a sermon or a song hit me as if it had been aimed directly at my consciousness. But the whole God-speaking-to-me-and-in-me thing has only happened three times. Once on the shore of that lake. Once when I was pregnant with Penny.[1] And once just before I met Peter.

I had organized a retreat to my grandparents' beach house. I invited a speaker to talk about Christianity, and I invited the entire school to come away for the night. I suspect the invitation to a beach house elicited more excitement than the promise of a religious message, but for whatever reason, forty-five students decided to come, including Peter Becker, who had never indicated any interest in spiritual things up to that point. The night went well—warm fall air and good pizza and a talk about how God loves us. By eleven o'clock, I was in my pajamas, ready to go to sleep. I was standing in a room full of people and it was as if all their chatter had been muted. I heard that voice again. This time it said, *Go find Peter Becker.*

I didn't want to listen. I didn't want to find Peter Becker. We had never even nodded in recognition in the hallway, and he had a bad reputation. I tried to ignore it. I walked upstairs to get ready for bed. *Go find Peter Becker*. I paused, and then I turned around and walked outside with a mustard-colored blanket wrapped around my shoulders. I found a group of my friends sitting in a circle around a small bonfire. *Go find Peter Becker.* I walked around to the front of the cottage, and there he was, with his back to me, jeans rolled up to his knees, standing alone in the water.

I never mustered up the courage to approach him. In fact, I turned away, praying now, asking what exactly I was supposed to say to this handsome young man to explain why I was stalking him in the dark. When I turned to go inside, I found him standing next to me, and I couldn't hold back the words, which were all of a sudden true: "I'm so happy you're here." Five and a half years later, he knelt down in that same spot, late at night. He asked me to marry him, and I said yes.

We've told our kids this story, and the other day, William said that God set us up on a blind date. That's certainly what it felt like, as if cosmic forces aligned to draw us to one another. Peter—the rebellious son of a single mother, with goals of joining a fraternity and then becoming an investment banker and making a million dollars before he was thirty. Me—the responsible eldest child of two eldest children, with goals of early admittance to an Ivy League university and work in a nonprofit or religious organization after that. Our families seemed so different. Our interest in each other seemed so unlikely. Not only that we met, but that we then stayed together through college at two different schools, with his home in New Orleans and mine in Connecticut, only underlined the providential nature of our relationship. At least, I've always thought of it that way.

I could tell much of my life story as a story of personal providence, of the notion that a loving God has been at work to make things work out well for me. Giving me a sense of purpose in the midst of my illness. Arranging for me to meet my future husband. Lining up a job for me right out of college. Providing a house that we could buy shortly after we got married. The list goes on. The capstone might have been when we decided to move away from Richmond, Virginia.

Peter had been working in a development role for a nonprofit, and he wanted to become a teacher in a boarding school. I had been working with high-school students—leading Bible discussion groups and giving chapel talks and otherwise continuing my Bible-beating ways, though hopefully in a more nuanced manner than the days of my early evangelical fervor—and I wanted to go to seminary so I could become a school chaplain. Princeton Seminary was my top choice. So we prayed that I would get into Princeton Seminary. And we prayed that Peter would get a job at a boarding school nearby. More specifically, we prayed he would get a job at Lawrenceville, the school closest to Princeton and, incidentally, the oldest and most established of the lot.

Peter did not have any teaching experience. He also did not have a master's degree, which many schools looked for.

He had coached soccer for high-school kids when he was in college, but his year of investment banking and then three years of fund-raising didn't demonstrate any obvious inclination or ability to spend his life in a classroom with a circle of earnest young intellectuals. He met with Lawrenceville's dean of faculty for an hour. They talked about mutual friends—the dean of admissions from our high school, who Peter had recently bumped into at a conference, the previous headmaster of Lawrenceville, who was a family friend of Peter's. They talked about Paris, where Peter and I had been given a trip recently by a local church. She asked him to come back two weeks later to interview with a series of faculty members.

On the morning we returned for his day of interviews—without ever asking anything about teaching or learning, without any other meeting—this same dean pulled Peter into her office and said, "The board of trustees is in town today, so I'm not going to be able to show you around as much as I might like. I am going to offer you the job, however, so you can just let me know at the end of the day if you'd like to take it." She laid out the terms—housing, health insurance, retirement benefits, and a low but decent salary. I had been admitted to Princeton Seminary a few weeks earlier. We saw no way to interpret these events as anything other than providence with a capital *P*. Answered prayer. It felt all the more God-given when, two months later, we learned that Peter's mom was sick with liver cancer, and we decided to move to New Orleans to care for her. It made sense: God had given us the security and stability of knowing where we were headed so that we could spend time with Peter's mom without worrying about the future, without the inconvenience and stress of interviews and résumés and flights back and forth. Then we put our house on the market and it sold, at a gain, in one weekend. We praised God.

I told this story—minus the religious interpretation of it—to one of Peter's colleagues at Lawrenceville a few years later, and she winced. "You know I love Peter," she said. "But I hate it when the good-old-boy network lets people skip the line."

With her words, an alternative reading of the events fell into place: Peter didn't get the job because of God or prayer. He got it because he looked the part. He literally wore the same gray pants, blue blazer, and Barbour jacket as the teacher who was the head of his department when he arrived on campus for that initial interview. Moreover, he knew the right people. He traveled in the right circles. He had married the right wife, the girl who also had a boarding-school background and an Ivy League degree. Maybe it wasn't providence that got him the job. Maybe it was privilege.

And if that experience was a result of privilege, what about meeting Peter in the first place? I had thought we were so different, but I later discovered that our grandparents had friends in common, that our mothers had cross-stitched the same patterns for us as infants, that our grandfathers had both graduated from Yale. Our upbringings ran a parallel course in more ways than we ever expected. We discovered that what we usually mean when we say "it's a small world" is that we travel in small circles. And what if the same could be said for other examples of answered prayer? What if privilege, more than providence, had ordered and defined my existence?

Stories in the Bible go back and forth between a God who loves and blesses all people—from the initial act of Creation to the final vision in the book of Revelation that promises a new heaven and a new earth for everyone under the sun—and a God who singles out certain groups and even certain individuals as "chosen." In the Old Testament, the Hebrew Bible, first Abraham and eventually the nation of Israel is called to be a people chosen by God. They are to worship God and God alone, and they will receive God's blessing. Disobedience and failure come next, and they experience some punishment, but this promise that they are chosen and beloved, and that God will bless them, loops through the prophets and poetry, the history and stories, a persistent reminder that God will be good to them, always and without fail, in spite of them.

The same thread runs through the New Testament, the part of the Bible that records stories about Jesus as well as the various letters to the early Christian churches to explain what being a Christian is all about. In these books we sometimes see individuals singled out—Jesus summons his disciples by name, Paul is blinded by a heavenly light on the road to Damascus—but Jesus' followers, both then and now, also hear that as a whole, they are chosen, beloved, blessed.

Whether we are talking about individuals or the whole community, it's tempting to read these passages of Scripture and interpret them as guarantees of an easy life. The American version of this reading has been dubbed the "prosperity gospel," a promise that trusting God will result in material provision, prayers answered the way we expect and desire.

But two other currents intersect the river of abundance in the Bible. One, the theme of suffering, the relentless insistence that God's people will be persecuted—like the Israelites enslaved in Egypt, exiled to Babylon, and later occupied by Rome; like Jesus' insistence, borne out in history, that following him would subject people to violence, scorn, and even grisly death. Two, there's the persistent message that God's blessing of particular individuals is a mechanism through which God can bless people in general. When God calls Abraham, God first promises that Abraham himself will be blessed, but then promises that "all nations" will be blessed through Abraham.[2] Similarly, when Jesus tells his followers to be "salt," he offers an image of a small particle that flavors and preserves food that would otherwise rot.[3] One teaspoon of salt is good for the whole piece of meat. God singles people out, God blesses, only so that the blessing can extend and abound.

There's a famous passage from Paul's letter to the Romans where he writes, "And we know that in all things God works for the good of those who love him, who have been called according to his purpose."[4] It's a lovely sentiment, the type that shows up on posters in Christian bookstores, the type I used to write on index cards and affix to my mirror. Paul's words seem to parallel the more secular but still quasi-spiritual idea that "everything happens for a reason." All things work for good. It sounds comforting, but I've cringed at the idea that everything has purpose, as if we can make sense of car accidents and heart attacks and suicide. Those words often have seemed to serve as a way to avoid the mystery of a world where not everything works out, where sometimes people are driven to despair, where suffering often appears to triumph. I think of my childhood friend Ben, who fell into a pool when he was four and stayed underwater for so long that when he came up he spent the rest of his life in a nursing home. Or of my friend Hannah, whose parents died together in a car crash one sunny afternoon. Or, on a far grander scale, of the Holocaust or the Rwandan genocide or the decimation of the Native American population when Europeans brought smallpox and guns to these shores. "Everything happens for a reason" discounts the presence of senseless evil in the world. And sometimes it seems as though the Christian faith does the same thing, as if everything from hunger to poverty to violence is somehow part of God's plan.

But the verses surrounding Paul's words in Romans describe a very different reality. In this passage, Paul meditates on suffering and hardship, on a world beset by death and enmity and hatred, on the situation in which Paul and other Christians find themselves, where professing faith in Jesus might very well lead to flogging, imprisonment, and execution. It's in this context that Paul talks about God being perpetually at work for good. Paul is not echoing the modern sentiment of everything happening for a reason. Instead, Paul seems to be saying that even the most senseless, purposeless, random, evil things cannot triumph over God's goodness, a goodness that is active, loving, purposeful, and patient. Everything that happens, the good and the bad, can be used by God, because that is how big God's goodness is, that is how inclusive and expansive and permanent God's goodness will be.

Which brings me back to that moment when I first heard God speaking to me, and to that moment when I first met Peter, and to Peter's job offer at Lawrenceville, and to all the other times I interpreted positive circumstances as God's blessing, God's affirmation, God's providence weaving together the disparate threads of my life. A part of me now feels cynical about my trusting assumptions that Peter got the job and I got into seminary—that we got the things we wanted—because God loved us and we prayed and it all worked out. An equally plausible explanation arises when I look at our résumés and personal connections and all the ways that privilege functions not only to get us what we want but even to make us think we earned those things, or that we were given them by God and not by social forces.

I think of the studies that have shown that when people apply for jobs, if their qualifications are identical but their name indicates they come from an African American cultural background, they are half as likely to get a callback as an applicant with a "white-sounding" name.[5] I think of my friend Romesh, a Sri Lankan who grew up in Atlanta,

Georgia, who despite his high GPA and scholarship to college and numerous varsity letters, was told repeatedly by his church youth-group peers and leaders that he shouldn't express any romantic interest in the white girls there due to a "biblical" mandate against interracial relationships. I think of my friend Patricia, who as an African American child in an otherwise white middle-school classroom was called "Nobody" by her teacher for an entire year. Romesh, Patricia, and I are all, if what the Bible says is true, equally loved by God. We are equally blessed. But we have not received equal treatment from other people.

I return to memories of dozens of small and large instances of blessing that I have attributed to God's provision and protection. I do not know whether those moments were evidence of the operation of privilege or stories of God's grace. But I am inclined to believe that God does not cause our suffering or our privilege. I am also inclined to believe that if God can use our suffering for good, God can also use our privilege for good.

Even if I wanted to, I could not rewrite the story of my life. I cannot unravel the threads of privilege and providence. With time, it has become all the more clear to me that affluence and the implicit benefits of whiteness do not come from my efforts, nor does my comfortable life come as a sign of God's favor resting upon me. But if I acknowledge the mystery rather than assuming my privilege has come as a direct result of God's blessing, then I can entrust that same privilege to God and pray that it be used for good, as a way to share the abundant blessings of a loving Creator. Like Paul, like Abraham, like Romesh and Patricia, like thousands of unknown saints throughout history, my life will be marked by events and social situations outside of my control. But I also long for it to be marked by a willingness to give myself, no matter the cost, to God's loving work in the world.

chapter nine

LOOKING UP

Two experiences of hardship have cut through my imaginary wall of privilege—my mother-in-law's diagnosis of liver cancer and her subsequent death, and the birth of her namesake, our daughter Penny, with her diagnosis of Down syndrome. The two events lie atop one another in my memory, like ancient ruins. Excavating each layer isn't precise. They fall into each other. They build upon one another. Together, they transformed the landscape of my heart.

I want to share these stories as a point of contact, as experiences that connect me to others through the common human currency of love and beauty and pain and sorrow. But I should also admit that I am tempted to use these tales of hardship as a shield. I imagine the criticism that can be lobbed my way as a person of great privilege, and I want to defend myself with protests that my life has not been as easy as it looks. I sometimes even want to launch an offensive, as if I can hurl my moments of suffering, my acts of self-sacrifice, toward a hypothetical foe who accuses me of ignorance or indifference or self-centeredness.

But I know that any time I jump to defend myself, and any time I want to attack, I do so because I am afraid. I am afraid that privilege has protected me from the harsh realities of everyday life, because even the hardships I have known have been mitigated by the facts of my whiteness and wealth and education. I am afraid that I don't know how to feel compassion. I am afraid that I will always be set apart from people who do not share my advantages. I am afraid that I am helpless to do anything about very real inequity and that sharing stories of personal suffering is a foil to distract from the reality of injustice. I am tempted to use hardship as a competitive ploy to prove my worth.

And yet it is also these experiences of pain and anger, of death and grief, and of hope and healing that have helped me to see both the allure of privilege and its false shimmer. It is these experiences of hardship that have helped me to yearn for a different type of privilege altogether.

When Peter and I were newly married and I was newly pregnant, we lived in a dormitory room in Rome for six weeks. The accommodations were simple: a linoleum floor, twin beds pulled together, an oscillating fan in the corner, a communal bathroom. Peter had received a Fulbright scholarship to study there, so he filled his days traveling with the other young teachers on the program—exploring ruins, reading ancient documents, and learning about the layers of history lying dormant below the buildings and streets and markets. I was a seminary student at the time, but that summer I decided to accompany him on this adventure and work on my first book, a memoir about caring for his mother when she had cancer. Each morning, Peter set out for another field trip, and I packed up some fruit and water and a legal pad and wandered the streets of Trastevere in search of a shady spot where I could write.

The setup sounds idyllic, but it was hot. My body was expanding due both to the new life within me and to the reality of our constant proximity to good pizza. My back hurt and my clothes tugged and I missed my friends and my provincial and predictable existence. I never found any gardens, and the local park had copious and intermittent piles of dog excrement on every path. Some days I abandoned my writing ambitions and instead walked myself to museums or monuments to see the treasures of the city. On my favorite outings, I successfully located a church with one minor masterpiece hanging in an altar. It was in one of these churches that I found Caravaggio's painting of the calling of Matthew. I knew the Bible story—Jesus singles out a wealthy tax collector as one of the men who would follow him to his death. In the painting, men cluster around a table, dressed as if they come from a royal court in Caravaggio's day. Light angles across the canvas in a diagonal line from Jesus' hand to Matthew's head, but Matthew doesn't look up. He is unaware of this unexpected intrusion, intent on counting the coins on the table.

I loved the visual intensity, the light and dark, the drama, but the painting did more than just tell the story of that initial encounter. My favorite aspect of it was Jesus' hand, index finger extended, a direct imitation of Michelangelo's depiction of Adam, the first human, on the ceiling of the Sistine Chapel. Caravaggio uses this simple gesture to tell us that Jesus is the second Adam, the one whose existence signals that God is re-creating the world, making it new. I loved the conversation between the artists, but I also loved the conversation Caravaggio was having with me, hundreds of years later. As if he wanted to tell me that every time Jesus calls someone, he is inviting them to be made new. In the painting, Matthew doesn't even see Jesus because he is poring over his money. But in the next frame, the frame of my imagination, Matthew looks up, astonished that this religious leader would single him out for something good. And then he surprises everyone by leaving his job, leaving his wealth, to follow Jesus.

In between the pizza and the art, I wrote in the courtyard behind our lodgings. I traveled back in my mind to the summer months two years earlier, when I had spent most of my days in my mother-in-law's air-conditioned living room in New Orleans, listening to her stories. We had moved in with her for the summer because she had recently been diagnosed with liver cancer. She had never remarried after her divorce from Peter's father twenty years earlier, so she needed practical help with wound care after surgery and meal preparation and the like. She also welcomed our company.

She often sat cross-legged in a loose white cotton nightgown that billowed around her, her short black hair now salt-and-pepper color, her big brown eyes still bright. I heard about summers in Biloxi, Mississippi—the biggest oak tree in the state shading their backyard swimming pool, the joy of playing cards and soaking in the sun on the beach, the devastating flooding of the family vacation home during Hurricane Camille. I heard about the people who loved her most—her grandmother and Rose, her nanny when she was a child. She told me about the trip to New York with her mother to buy a white satin gown covered with pounds of glimmering stones for her debut into society as a Queen of Mardi Gras. She also told me about wanting to forgive, all these years later, the priest who had sexually abused her as a teenager. And then one day she asked if I would share with her some Bible verses about heaven. "I want to know more about where I'm going," she said.

I wrote down verses on index cards, visions of a future with a God who would "prepare a place for [us],"[1] a God who longed to bless us with "life . . . to the full,"[2] a God who promised "no more . . . mourning or crying or pain."[3] When I handed her the cards, she lowered her eyes and slumped into her chair and said, "I've done so many things wrong," as if the words of blessing and life could not apply to her. I told her the story of the thief hanging on the cross next to

Jesus, the one who knew he deserved to die a criminal's death but who reached out to Jesus anyway. I said, "Even his crimes weren't enough to drive away Jesus' love. Even for him, Jesus promised, 'Today you will be with me in paradise.'"[4]

I wandered the cement streets of Rome two years later, new life announcing itself in my body, marveling at the Pantheon, the Trevi Fountain, the Dome of St. Peter's, holding the memories of love and loss. Being with my mother-in-law throughout her illness had forced me to reckon with a deeper level of suffering than I had ever encountered before. There was the physical reality of holding a trash can while she vomited, draining her tubes of blood and bile after her surgery, spending the night by her side in the hospital to make sure she didn't lurch from her bed. There was the sadness I carried simply from hearing her stories, the years of hurt that piled on top of her and pressed her down. And there was the spiritual conflict spurred by the age-old questions surrounding death. But intertwined with the pain and the grief was the healing.

My mother-in-law's sickness brought her to life, as if she had been like Matthew in the painting, looking down and counting the coins, and then the cancer had snapped her head to attention and she saw for the first time that the love of God had reached out, had singled her out, had pointed straight at her heart. She, like Matthew, said an unexpected yes. And everything changed. Friends and family rallied around her—cleaning out closets and accompanying her to doctors' appointments, bringing food and flowers and books and cards and laughter and memories and tears. She told people how much she loved them. She forgave and asked for forgiveness.

A week or so before she died, we took a walk outside. She wore that same white nightgown. Her hair was matted to her head. She took unsteady steps on the cracked and uneven pavement of a city constructed on water. She clasped my arm and said, "There will be music and dancing." Her thoughts didn't always line up those days, with the toxins building in her body and brain, the pain medication making everything inside fuzzy and slow. But I think she was talking about heaven. *There will be music. And dancing.*

Twice while we were in Rome, I went to see a midwife. She weighed me and listened to the baby's heartbeat and checked my vital signs and patted me on the back with a smile as I stood up and walked out into the bright sunlight. In August, in the middle of the night, I felt the flutter of the little one within me for the first time. I smiled in the darkness. It would be weeks before I could share the sensation, even with Peter. For now, that life was mine alone, expanding within me, relying upon me, and reaching out to me in return.

As soon as we landed in the United States, I saw my doctor. She offered me a routine blood test. A quad screen, she called it. I asked if it would affect the baby. "All it will do is give you information about potential abnormalities," she said. I stuck out my arm and gave the blood. She called back a few days later. According to the bloodwork, I had a small chance—1 in 313, to be precise—of having a baby with Down syndrome. What did I want to do? When I explained that I wouldn't want to terminate the pregnancy even if our baby did have Down syndrome, she suggested a Level 2 ultrasound, just to be sure the baby was healthy. I scheduled the ultrasound for the following week. I didn't think much of it. I was twenty-eight years old, and this pregnancy had been easy, and 1 in 313 seemed very unlikely to me.

A few days later, we reported to the hospital. The baby wriggled and kicked, and we could tell by the lightness of the technician's manner that she saw a healthy kid. She confirmed our thoughts with the words, "This baby may be many things. But it does not have Down syndrome." We asked her to write down our baby's sex for us. In the parking lot, we opened the envelope to read, "Buy pink! It's a girl!" Right then and there, we named her for her grandmother. We named her Penny, and we celebrated the good news.

When she was growing within me, I wondered what aspects of her grandmother Penny would inherit—her love for massages and manicures and beautiful things? Her high cheekbones and strong jawline? Her exuberance when consuming decadent treats like Häagen-Dazs ice cream or filet mignon?

But then our daughter Penny was born, and soon thereafter the doctors told us they suspected she had Down syndrome after all. For a time, we grieved the loss of the child we had thought we were bringing into the world. And at first, the grief felt familiar. I remembered the day when Peter's mother couldn't get out of bed anymore, when her skin glowed yellow with jaundice, when purple marks appeared on her forearms. I traveled in my mind to her death, that moment of dramatic departure that came after days in an agitated coma, as if every breath were a fight. When she died, the men left the room, and the women—her sisters, her daughters-in-law, her best friends—washed her body. Her skin was stained with brown fluid. We caressed her shoulders with sponges. We sprinkled her flesh with lavender oil. We found a clean white nightgown and pulled it over her head. We combed her hair. It felt sacred, like heaven and earth touched for a moment, like the edges of life had become permeable.

That sense of sacredness and sorrow returned when I gave birth to her namesake. Our daughter did not inherit her grandmother's cheekbones or her aesthetic sensibilities. But like her grandmother, Penny's life opened us up to vulnerability, to both pain and beauty. Human need drew us into human connection. Penny's life opened up possibilities we had never previously explored, possibilities for life and healing and hope beyond hope, for a world in which money and achievement and physical appearance fade in comparison to friendship and forgiveness and love.

Without Grand Penny's death, I don't know how I would have been able to receive her granddaughter's life. With her cancer diagnosis, we faced a problem that all our intellectual tools and high-powered connections and financial wherewithal could not solve. We were forced to move past those surface answers to a world where suffering is part of our common humanity. We were forced to enter into grief, which also allowed us to enter into gratitude for the present moment—for the way the light falls upon the water at sunset, for the feel of this soft hand holding mine, for forgiveness of the hurts of the past, for the hope of eventual reunion. Penny's death taught me that the hardships we would never invite can bring transformation we would never reject. When our daughter was born with a diagnosis that seemed like a hardship in its own right, for her and for me, I looked back to her namesake and sensed that once again, this vulnerable and unpredictable life we had been given would grow us up and bring both joy and beauty. Without the experience of Penny's death, when our daughter Penny was born, I, too, might have been like Matthew in Caravaggio's painting, counting the coins of my existence, unable or unwilling to look up into the light.

In both of these experiences, our position of privilege helped us in some ways. We had money to pay for plane tickets to and from New Orleans, and we could manage for a few months without an income. We had access through Peter's family to medical attention others might not have received. Our educational backgrounds gave us confidence in talking with doctors and advocating for ourselves with insurance companies. With our daughter Penny, our privilege has again set her apart in some ways from her peers with Down syndrome. We have lived in towns with tax bases that provide for excellent special-education programs in the public schools. We have been able to afford to have one parent work part time in order to manage doctor's appointments and help with homework and drive to ballet class. Still, these experiences of hardship taught me about a different type of privilege than that afforded through money and skin color.

Privilege means being given a special status—legal or social—by virtue of something you didn't earn. Privilege means being undeservedly yet unquestionably singled out. The way we typically assign privilege—based on race or gender or religion or economic status—distorts our humanity. It cuts us off from one another. But in those times of hardship, I experienced a different kind of privilege, a kind of unearned beauty and promise and grace that did not emerge from anything having to do with wealth or education or ethnicity. I experienced the privilege of holding my mother-in-law's hand while she slept, of singing when she was anxious and watching her body calm, of praying in the midst of her wordless moans and realizing that she needed her sons to be by her side when she died. It wasn't the privilege of social or legal status. It wasn't the privilege of affluence. It was the privilege of being singled out for something purposeful, being the undeserving recipient of the gift of human connection.

It was that same sense of privilege that came when I talked to a new father of a baby with Down syndrome, and he asked me whether his daughter would ever know him as her father, and I could send assurance across the telephone lines. The same sense of privilege when Penny and I used to go to our local Panera for lunch, and a young woman who worked there would go out of her way to attend to us, offering free cookies and clearing our table without asking. One day she said, "Your daughter reminds me of my sister back in Morocco. I miss her so much." And suddenly I had more in common with this young immigrant from Morocco who understood my love for my daughter than I did with anyone else in that restaurant. "My sister's name is Doha," she told us.

Sometimes I think about privilege in terms of times I have been overcome by gratitude, when I have recognized the undeserved moments of beauty and grace and purpose that connect instead of divide. The list unfurls: The time I swayed with the music in a multicultural worship service. The time I folded sheets and towels for my best friend after her brother died. The time I rocked a friend's newborn baby to sleep. The time I passed out the Communion wafers at my grandmother's funeral and was entrusted with the words, "This is the body of Christ, broken for you."

The privilege of whiteness and wealth can become a wall against the privilege of being human, loved not for status or performance but simply loved, and able to give love in return not because of obligation but in grateful response to an invitation. I have been given much that I do not deserve, and my very real social privilege has cut me off from others as much as it has also made my life comfortable. But social privilege is not the end of my story. The real privilege of my life has come in learning what it means to love others, that love involves suffering and sacrifice and sleepless nights and tears and heartache and great gifts.

It makes sense to talk about privilege in terms of access to private clubs and schools and bank loans and preferential treatment by authorities. It makes sense to expose the injustices of privilege and call for them to be rectified. But there is also the privilege of cleaning the wounds of people you love, of participating in healing and new life, of becoming vulnerable and needy and receiving love and care. There is another type of privilege, privilege that connects instead of divides, that shimmers through the air like a line of light, available if only we stop counting the coins and look up.

chapter ten

BELOVED

Penny and I head into Target with a mission: Advil, long-sleeved T-shirts, and a wall calendar. But Penny stops short after we walk through the automatic doors. She casts a furtive glance at a young man and his mother standing nearby. I follow her eyes and wonder if I know what she's thinking. I take her hand and start walking. I don't want them to catch us staring. She turns around to look over her shoulder. Then she does it again. A few minutes later, when we are out of their earshot, I ask her, "Penny, what did you notice about that man with the orange sweatshirt?"

Her eyes widen. "He has Down syndrome!" she says.

"That's right," I nod in agreement. "How did you know?"

"Well, he's wearing glasses and his tongue sticks out."

We are now strolling hand in hand down the medicine aisle. Though Penny is ten years old, she is small for her age. Her light brown hair cups her round face. Her pink-rimmed glasses hide the green and yellow and blue sparkle of her eyes. I pluck the Advil from the shelf.

We find the rest of our items and proceed to the checkout line. Penny slides the credit card through the machine and pushes the green button and signs an approximation of my name. After we load our purchases into the trunk, Penny takes her customary position in the car—behind the passenger seat so she has a good view of the driver. I adjust the rearview mirror so I can see her face, and I ask, "How did it feel to see another person with Down syndrome?"

She shrugs and turns her head to the side. I wait. Then her eyes catch mine and I see the beginnings of a smile. "It's kind of cool," she says, in a voice barely above a whisper.

Penny pulls a book out of the "book bin" we keep in the car and begins to read. I plug in my headset, but I pause before I push Play on my audiobook. We've talked about Down syndrome for all of Penny's life, but she's never noticed another person with the condition before. I smile with relief at her excitement in making that unspoken connection. I wonder whether she will identify more and more with other people with Down syndrome as she enters adolescence.

I imagine it will be complicated. Penny sees Down syndrome as positive right now, but she may see it differently in her teenage years. I know older women with Down syndrome who see their disability as negative. Penny may struggle with being outside the circle of what is considered "normal" when it comes to height, appearance, and ability.

Thinking about whatever process Penny will go through to understand her own identity makes me think about how contested the idea of identity is right now, and how her own growing self-awareness might align with the struggles around identity expressed by other marginalized groups. Protests and conflicts have erupted from the political arena to the courts to college classrooms. At Yale University, the touchpoint was Halloween: First the administration asked students to be sensitive when selecting costumes. Then Erika Christakis, a faculty-in-residence, wrote an email suggesting that students should not be censored by the university, even if their costumes were insensitive or racist. She said she was promoting freedom of speech and community engagement, not condoning or in any way supporting the potentially offensive costumes. Protests, and eventually her resignation, ensued. At Evergreen College in Washington State, a self-described liberal professor wrote a letter of protest when white people were asked to leave campus for a "Day of Absence." The backlash included bomb threats, and the professor in question went into hiding. Other protests ranged from Middlebury College in Vermont to the University of California, Berkeley, and they all circled around questions of identity—white, black, gay, straight, conservative, liberal, disabled, able-bodied. The protests underscore the confusion in our nation about how we define who we are, and about whether those definitions will always be in conflict with one another. They bring up the question of whether identity is always about power and privilege, about some group being oppressed and another asserting superiority. I long for a way to understand identity that allows for diversity and particularity without necessitating division.

Penny interrupts my thoughts. "Mom, can we just talk?"

"Sure, sweetie," I say. "What do you want to talk about?"

"My birthday." Her birthday is eight months away, but Penny tends to cycle through a familiar series of topics, and planning a celebration of her life is a common theme of our car rides together. We discuss frozen yogurt, movies, and trampoline parks, and then she returns to her book and I to my contemplation.

My position of cultural privilege has insulated me from the hurt that can come from having an identity that is outside the norm. Were it not for Penny's presence in my life, I might still feel dismissive or at least bewildered by the controversies. But now we have been on the receiving end of insensitive comments—whether by friends who call themselves "retarded" for dropping a fork at a dinner party or on a public bus with a group of rambunctious teenagers throwing the same insult at one another. Or even when reading. Kate DiCamillo's *Because of Winn-Dixie* is one of our favorite books. It tells the story of Opal, a lonely little girl who rescues an abandoned dog and befriends all sorts of unexpected characters in her small southern town. But I flinched when

I was reading it out loud to the kids and some boys called Opal's friend "retarded." The ugliness of the outside world had intruded. I wished we had been warned.

As I have learned more about the history of people with intellectual disabilities, I have seen the parallels in their treatment to that of other oppressed groups. Just as Jewish people were singled out by the Nazis, so, too, were children with Down syndrome. If we had lived in Nazi Germany, our daughter would have been taken away and killed, and we would have been powerless to stop it.[1] And just as women of color have suffered a long history of sexual assault at the hands of white men with little or no recourse, recent government data shows that people with intellectual disabilities are seven times more likely to be victims of sexual assault than the general population.[2] For all the ways in which Penny can identify as a person of privilege, she is also aligned with people who have been marginalized and oppressed through the centuries.

I still believe college students need to be introduced to the hard topics of racism and sexism. I believe speech—even hateful, awful, ugly speech—needs protection in order for democracy to flourish. But I am increasingly able to understand the rawness of being on the receiving end of a statement of animosity and of a history of exclusion. In the midst of the discord, I want to advocate for a different way to construct identity, a way that makes room for grace and forgiveness and healing. A way that allows for "safe spaces" without walling ourselves off from one another.

I spend the car ride home lost in these thoughts. Penny mutters the words to *Tales of a Fourth Grade Nothing* under her breath. For as many hours as she reads every day, reading in her head still feels too challenging.

We arrive home, and I unload the bags while Penny unpacks her backpack. "Do you have any homework?" I ask.

"Nope," she says.

"Well, are you working on anything at school these days?"

"Research," she says.

I have learned to wait for more information instead of peppering her with questions. I hang the calendar on the wall next to the refrigerator and put the plastic bags in the cupboard.

She climbs onto a stool at the kitchen island and says, "Big questions. Like, my 'big question' is 'Why is Down syndrome scary?'"

I stop moving for a moment, my back to her, my throat suddenly tight.

She says, "I know you were scared when I was born. But I don't know why."

I nod, allowing her words to take me back to those early days. I once compared the way I felt to a woman standing on a beach before a tsunami, watching the water recede, knowing a wave was coming, and knowing she could do nothing to stop it. But the fear that once swept over me like surf pounding a rocky beach is hard to even conjure in my imagination anymore. *Why is Down syndrome scary?*

Some of my fear was for Penny's health, but even once

the medical concerns had been alleviated, the fear remained. In some ways, Penny's "big question" might as well be *Why is difference scary?*

"Down syndrome isn't scary to me anymore," I offer, turning to face her.

She holds my gaze for a moment and nods. "Can I have some nachos?" she asks.

Together we assemble the chips and cheese. She heats them up in the microwave and munches with contentment. I'm still thinking about this afternoon—about who she is becoming and about how she has taught me to understand identity differently than I once did, both hers and mine.

Penny's arrival in our lives pushed the question of human identity into the forefront of my mind. Was my identity the same as our daughter's? Or were we fundamentally different from one another? I went back to philosophical arguments from college about what makes us human. Did our humanity arise from the capacity to reason—*I think, therefore I am*—in which case people with severe intellectual disabilities, or people who haven't had access to Western school systems, might be considered less than human? Did our humanity arise from our capacity for laughter, our ability to create art, our toolmaking, our capacity for language?

None of those answers satisfied me, so I turned to the early pages of the book of Genesis. This ancient Hebrew text states it clearly and simply: Both male and female were created "in the image of God."[3] Figuring out what it means to be created in the image of God has prompted much theological debate, but I am inclined to believe we overthink it. There are dozens of names for God throughout the Bible and dozens of attributes used to describe God, but God is equated with a single concept only once, in a letter written to the early church by John. "God is love," John writes.[4] God's nature—for all its complexity and inscrutability—can be stated succinctly: love.

Penny eats in silence as I wash the remaining breakfast and lunch dishes. I wonder whether it really could be that simple: Human beings, as God's "image bearers," are created to receive and reflect God's love. From the beginning of the human story, at least according to Genesis, humans are those who are loved by God and called to love others. Love is who we are and who we are meant to be. Love is what makes us human.

When I encounter someone with whom I do not have an easy affinity, someone different from me by virtue of age or religion or economics or ability, I want to remember what we hold in common, that we both bear the image of God, the image of love. That reminder doesn't change our differences or eliminate the markers of our respective identities. It doesn't make me "color-blind." Rather, it opens me up to the possibility that in this human being who is different from me, I can see and learn and grow and receive and give back to the love that fuels our existence.

A voice in my head argues that I am oversimplifying things. A cynic might roll his eyes at my abstract and idealistic portrait of humanity. Christians could easily do the same, because I haven't acknowledged the dark side of human nature, what religious people call sin. Indeed, just a few pages beyond the Bible's description of the glorious creation of human beings comes the scene in which those two original image-bearers of God chose to turn away from love and toward themselves.[5] We humans have been repeating their pattern ever since. I used to think of sin as immoral actions, but I have come to think of it as much more than that. I now think of sin as everything that separates us from love. That's why I often use the word *brokenness* instead of *sin* to describe everything in me and in the world around me that doesn't line up with love. Sometimes that brokenness arises from an action for which I am responsible—I cause fissures in relationships when I lie or say mean things about someone else, for example. But other things—like war or mental illness—can separate us from love even when we have no control over them.

Broken and beloved—these truths of my identity connect me to every human being who walks this earth. If I start to see people who seem radically different from me as those who instead are radically similar to me—needy, broken, with the potential for beauty and joy and glory—then love could begin to connect us, and fear would not be able to divide us. Love could hold us together.

These two poles of human existence—sin and love—seem to be in constant tension with one another. If anything, when I look at the newspaper headlines, I might think sin has the upper hand in identifying who we are as a human race. But before sin entered the world, God—which is to say,

Love—existed. Love existed from before the beginning, and love exists eternally. Sin is an interlude, an interloper, a torrid distraction from the love of God. Christians believe that Jesus overcame sin through an act of sacrificial love. The power of sin was broken by love. Love remains. As much as brokenness defines our identities and our world right now, deeper still is our common identity as those who are loved.

Penny finishes her snack and brings her plate over to add to the dishes. I turn off the water and call after her, "Hey Pen, you know your big question? Do you have an answer yet?"

She shakes her head. "Not yet."

I bite the inside of my lip. *Why is Down syndrome scary?* She is doing her own research. She hasn't asked for my response. But I want her to know that the fear has receded, leaving me instead with this kind and earnest daughter, this unexpected treasure after the storm.

I check in with Penny about her research over the next few weeks. She learns about extra chromosomes and low muscle tone and some of the distinguishing features of Down syndrome. But she never answers her big question. Perhaps one day she will understand why we felt the way we did, or maybe it will always bewilder her that we were engulfed by fear when we were presented with the gift of her life.

She is on the cusp of seeing herself not only as a girl who belongs to this family and this town and this church, but also as a part of the Down syndrome community. She tells me she would like to meet more kids her age who have Down syndrome. She writes a postcard to another little girl with Down syndrome and asks, "Do you like having a disability?" She is beginning to explore the ways that her body and brain and genetic code are distinct, and she may well one day identify herself first and foremost as a member of the disability community. But my hope is that the foundation of her identity is the love that was bestowed upon her from the moment of her creation. If she can believe that love is the core of who she is and how she has been made, then she will know the freedom to discover her gifts, her limitations, and even her brokenness without fear.

Penny gives a presentation in class about her "big question." Her teacher emails me to say she did a great job and also to report that many of her classmates were confused. They didn't know Penny had something different about her. That night, as I tuck her in, Penny looks up at me, her eyes unobstructed by her glasses, a sleepy smile on her face. She holds my hand and insists upon a hug and a kiss. "Every five minutes," she says—a long-standing and unrealized hope that I will check on her regularly until she's asleep. "Every five minutes," I say, even though it is a promise I do not always keep.

But tonight I come back. Even while she sleeps, I can see that she has Down syndrome. And even while she sleeps, I can see that she is my daughter. She is just starting to discover her own identity, but a decade ago she pushed me to recognize the ways I had constructed an identity based on a false self—based on the intelligence and abilities and cultural background that set me apart from others rather than recognizing the personhood that had been bestowed upon me and upon every other human being I have the privilege to encounter. It is because of Penny that I have begun to believe that what we all hold in common is love.

chapter eleven

POSSIBILITIES

I probably shouldn't be surprised to learn that Penny is one of four kids to advance to the all-school spelling bee. Penny has always loved words. As a preschooler, she would ask us to give her big words to say out loud. In the evenings, Peter and I meandered around campus with Penny and William side by side in their double jogger stroller, Penny's little voice repeating back to us words like *onomatopoeia, ridiculous, symphony, brontosaurus, ontological.* Her speech was incomprehensible to any outside listener, but we took great joy in her attempts to enunciate. Then, once she reached elementary school and learned to read, it became our habit during car rides to give each other words to spell. Easy words came first—*bed, hat, tin, cap*. And then "medium words" like *mailbox, evergreen, point, basket.* Finally, "medium-hard words" that kept us giggling with the letters she would mix up from the back seat: *hospital, telephone, beautiful.*

Still, when Penny buries her face in my lap with the news that she will be in the school spelling bee, I almost cry with surprise and pride and excitement for her. I didn't even know the school had a spelling bee, much less that Penny would have a chance to be in it. She practices every night. Say the word, spell the word, say the word. Think about it first. Say it slowly. Have fun. She lies on the couch with the list of practice words. *Peculiar, fluoroscope, forewarn, generous.*

On the day of the competition, ten kids line up in their chairs in the front of the auditorium. Penny, legs dangling, smaller than anyone else, sits up straight with a big smile. She spots me and waves. The first round consists of three words. She spells the first one wrong: *rarely*, with two *l*'s. She spells the second one wrong: *surprise*, without the second *r*. But she gets her final word right. She marches with confidence to the microphone. She says the word, spells the word, says the word. "Possible. P-O-S-S-I-B-L-E. Possible."

Penny sits down in the audience after that round along with three of her peers, and she cheers for the kids who advance to the second round and then to the final. I feel as though I have additional capacity inside my chest, as if my delight in our daughter—her love for language, her confidence, her excitement for other students—has suddenly become too big for me to contain.

The story of Penny's whole life is a story of possibilities, and yet parents of so many vulnerable kids like her—children who grow up in poverty or other unstable environments, children with medical conditions and disabilities—are told from early on that what they dream for the future is impossible. Studies have shown that teachers interpret African American boys as more threatening than their white peers, at least in part because they see these boys as older than they actually are. These boys are more regularly suspended and even expelled from classrooms, often beginning a cycle of punishment and negative consequences.[1] Other studies have shown that girls perform worse in athletic contests when they are reminded of the stereotype that girls are less physically capable than boys.[2] All of these kids are subject to what columnist and former presidential speechwriter Michael Gerson called "the soft bigotry of low expectations."[3] Penny's story at the spelling bee stands as an immediate and concise counterpoint, evidence of what is indeed possible.

But Penny's success at the spelling bee shouldn't be what demonstrates her worth to the rest of the world. Penny's "success" didn't emerge out of a need to prove herself. It didn't emerge out of a competitive spirit. And it didn't emerge out of a belief that if she could demonstrate her abilities, then she would be rewarded. Penny's achievements at the spelling bee, such as they were, emerged out of the delight she received from reading and word games. Her confidence emerged out of love, whether she was aware of it or not. She really does love spelling. But deeper than that, Penny has been loved—by her parents, by her teachers and friends and neighbors and babysitters and, first and foremost, by God.

Around the same time Penny was born, the dean of faculty at the school where Peter taught began to reference a psychologist named Carol Dweck, who studied the difference between kids, parents, and teachers who operated according to a "growth" mindset or a "fixed" mindset.[4] For Peter, the implications of this research had as much to do with our baby daughter as they did with any student in his humanities class. Dweck concludes that many of us grow up with presuppositions—assumptions handed to us from family members, teachers, or the culture at large—about what we are "good" at, about our "natural" abilities, and about the areas in which we can, or cannot, succeed. When we treat those presuppositions as if they are prophetic announcements, we develop a "fixed" mindset. We end up thinking things like "I'm not good at math," because I got a C on a test or because learning the material felt challenging or because I'm a girl. Or we think, "My child will never get a job," because that child didn't complete a task on time, or because he failed a class at school, or because she has a disability. We end up categorizing ourselves and those around us: smart, pretty, athletic, stubborn, dramatic, emotional.

Dweck's research demonstrates that virtually every person can grow in areas of perceived weakness, as long as they assume growth is indeed possible. She never uses words like "beloved" to describe people with "growth" mindsets, and yet love—the love of God, yes, but even the love of a parent for a child or a teacher for a student, of anyone who looks in from the outside and says, "You are valuable because of who you are and not because of what you can do"—that kind of love opens us up to discover all sorts of possibilities.

In the years after Penny was born, I read book after book about disability and human vulnerability. In one of them, *The Power of the Powerless*, Christopher de Vinck writes about growing up with his brother, who had been born with significant cognitive disabilities. De Vinck describes his brother to a classroom of students, and one of them says, "Oh . . . you mean he was a vegetable." De Vinck responds, "Well, I guess you could call him a vegetable. I called him Oliver, my brother."[5] Oliver de Vinck never spoke. He never walked or ran. But his family loved him. They experienced love in return.

I recently read a pair of books, *Tattoos on the Heart* and *Barking to the Choir*, by Father Greg Boyle,[6] a Franciscan priest who works largely with young men of color who are involved in gangs in Los Angeles. In story after story, Boyle relates reciprocal relationships of love with these young men, whom he calls homies. He writes about homies from rival gangs who work side by side and become friends. Homies who become tenderhearted fathers. One homie who is in the hospital and can hardly move but wants to hear from Father Greg how he is handling his cancer treatment. *But YOU, G? How are YOU doing?* he writes on a sheet of paper when he is too beat up from a car accident to open his mouth. Greg Boyle humanizes these men whom our society looks at as hardened criminals because he demonstrates their capacity to give and receive love.

Understanding love as the basis of human identity changes the social fabric for kids like Penny. Love allowed Christopher de Vinck to see his brother very differently than the student in his classroom. Love changed the way Greg Boyle saw the young men in his community, and once they began to believe in his love and in God's love for them, those same young men were able to grow and change and give back. But it isn't only people on the margins who need to understand their belovedness. People with privilege—and I include myself here—also crave the knowledge that we are loved, not for what we do but for who we are, loved simply because we were formed and guided by Love.

William is in third grade now, and he is beginning to work on a project on China. He starts by trying to create a three-dimensional map of the tallest buildings in the country, but it is hard to coax Lego pieces into the structures he envisions. One afternoon he hurls his construction across the room and runs upstairs. I find him in his bed. His face holds a mix of anger and defeat. He, too, needs to know that he is loved for who he is and not for what he can do. I see myself in my son, and I know that plenty of other kids face their own inclination to give up and feel like a failure as soon as an assignment becomes challenging, as soon as their performance doesn't meet their own high standards.

I am working on a series of reflections for a school up in New Hampshire. The chaplain there has invited me to talk with six hundred high school students about what I've learned during more than a decade as Penny's mom. One morning, after I drop the kids off at school, I turn on a podcast; *On Being* host Krista Tippett is interviewing poet Michael Longley. He gets my attention immediately when he says, "One of the marvelous things about poetry is that it's useless. It's useless." He pauses for effect, and then continues, "'What use is poetry?' people occasionally ask. . . . And the answer is no use, but it doesn't mean to say that it's without value. It's without use, but it is valuable."[7]

Longley's words lead me to think about what poetry has to offer—beauty, peace, insight into the human condition, questions about meaning and purpose, a connection to something transcendent and bigger than ourselves. And then my mind moves from poetry to people. I think of Penny first—many individuals with disabilities, many elderly people, many people living in poverty, do not contribute in any measurable economic way to our society. *Useless*, some might say. *A burden. A drain*. And from a purely material, utilitarian way of thinking, they might be right. But Longley's words make me think about myself, about Marilee and William, and about the students I will speak to next week. Understanding love as the basis of human identity, understanding the value of every human being, independent of work or achievement, is a truth we all need to hear.

When I arrive at the chapel, I walk into a soaring space with wooden pews and Gothic arches. The students in the choir scurry around in long black and white robes as the notes from a complicated organ fugue surround us. Thirty minutes later, the rest of the students and faculty file in—many with their hair still wet, coming straight to this service after athletic practices and a quick shower. They giggle and chatter and nudge each other as they settle into their seats. I can only assume that most of them are not eagerly anticipating this required religious service wedged between a long day of work and the dinner and free time that awaits.

I take my place at the high wooden lectern and look out at row after row of pristine faces. The boys wear ties and blue blazers, the girls skirts or dresses. I share with them the Michael Longley quotation about value and usefulness, and I admit that I often conflate the two. I thoughtlessly assume that without usefulness—without demonstrable physical and intellectual abilities that could lead to financial productivity in the future—our lives hold no value. And then I tell them about Penny, about how my love for her helped me to understand her value.

I say, "Imagine meeting someone who doesn't care about your grades or what college you're going to or what exclusive internship you got for the summer. Imagine that person seeing beneath all the layers of achievement and loving you."

I look out at a sea of teenagers with "potential," with impressive college prospects and hours of community service and grand ambitions that they may well realize. I know that many of them walk around, like I did when I was in their shoes, with a deep longing to know that it is not their performance that brings them worth. It is not their achievement that makes them lovable. I want these kids to be free from the relentless need to prove themselves. I want them to be able to explore what they love and not simply achieve what they are good at. I want them to be able to rest.

"Having a child with disabilities has expanded my capacity to love and value others, but it has also expanded my ability to believe that I am loved not because of my achievements but because of my humanity, in all my vulnerabilities and weaknesses and beauty and gifts. You, too, are limited and needy, gifted and glorious. And your value comes not because of your SAT scores or your likelihood of becoming an investment banker someday. Your value—like Penny's, like mine—comes because you are known and you are loved, with a love that is patient and kind, a love that always hopes, always protects, always trusts, always perseveres. Our value comes because we are loved by a love that never fails."

I scan their faces one more time, and I am surprised to see the tears trickling down some of their cheeks. I am surprised by their rapt attention. I am surprised by how much we all need to know that we are valuable not because of our usefulness but because we are loved.

I see Penny's life as a signpost. Penny's abilities have emerged out of the supports she has received, but those abilities have also emerged out of love. She makes me believe that kids who are growing up in poverty, or who have learning disabilities, or intellectual disabilities, or genetic conditions that make them more vulnerable, or kids who carry the undeserved weight of prejudice because of their ethnicity or gender or religion—that possibilities for joy and connection and love and purpose exist for all. Penny also makes me believe that the kids who are suffocating from the pressure cooker of achievement can find rest and peace and purpose. If we believed that all children are beloved human beings, maybe we would be more inclined as a society to give them the opportunities to discover their abilities, their gifts. Maybe we would invest not only financial resources but also time and prayer and hope for their futures. Maybe we wouldn't need them to prove their usefulness if we believed in their value.

When I was a student myself, I learned that the best way to argue a point was from an objective perspective. The knowledge that mattered was rational knowledge. Prioritizing rational knowledge has led to scientific advances and great insights and learning. It has also led to movements like eugenics in the early twentieth century, when scientific "proof" buttressed anti-Semitism and racism and sexism and the forced sterilization of people with intellectual disabilities. This strain of thinking continues even now with the assumption that people with low IQs suffer implicitly, presumably by virtue of their inability to gain the same knowledge as their peers from a typical classroom education. But Eastern spiritual traditions as well as the Judeo-Christian Scriptures see knowledge differently. For the apostle Paul, rational knowledge is subservient to love. Paul writes to the Philippians, "This is my prayer: that your love may abound more and more in knowledge and depth of insight,"[8] and to the Galatians, "The only thing that counts is faith expressing itself through love,"[9] and to the Ephesians, Paul prays that they would be able to grasp the "love that surpasses knowledge."[10] He writes to the Corinthians, "If I have . . . all knowledge . . . but do not have love, I am nothing."[11]

The intellect counts for nothing unless it is informed by love.

I used to wonder if my love for Penny clouded my judgment of ethical issues related to Down syndrome. But Paul's words convince me that I can see Penny clearly only because I love her, that I can see myself clearly only when I believe that I am loved, that Christopher de Vinck saw his brother clearly and Father Greg sees the men in his neighborhood clearly because they love them. I have started to believe that love is the only lens that matters when it comes to our knowledge of other human beings.

Over the course of her fifth-grade year at school, Penny's principal decides to instill the traits of a growth mindset throughout the student body. Carol Dweck's research that Peter had first learned about a decade earlier is now summarized in posters in the hallway and discussed in community meetings. One afternoon, Penny is watching Marilee as she starts to ride a bike with no training wheels. Marilee topples over and stands up in frustration. "I can't do it!" she says, her whole body tense with what looks like the desire to throw her bike as far away from her as possible.

From the porch, Penny yells, "Marilee. Put on your growth mindset! You can't do it . . . yet!"

It doesn't matter that Penny can spell the word *possible*. But it does matter that we understand that all our lives are filled with possibilities, and that those possibilities emerge out of an identity rooted and established in love.

chapter twelve

NECESSARY ACTION

When William turns eight, a friend gives him a paperback copy of *Where the Red Fern Grows* as a birthday present. Peter and I both remember the book from our childhoods, and we compete for turns to read the story of Billy, a young boy in the country hills of Oklahoma, who saves his money to buy two young dogs and then trains them to become the best coon hunters in the area. Every night at bedtime, our kids gather around to hear what happens next—whether Billy will succeed in his fight against the local bully, whether his family will have enough money for their basic needs, and whether he will win the prize for the best hunting dogs in the state. As we near the end, Peter is away for work for a few nights, so I take the spot on the middle of the couch, book in hand. The drama intensifies—during the hunt, Billy's grandfather, who has been his biggest supporter through these years of growing up with his dogs, breaks his leg. They face impossible weather conditions of ice and fog. It looks like certain defeat. And yet, despite these trials, Billy and his dogs ultimately emerge victorious. Billy wins more money than his family has ever had. They can now look forward to a better life. They anticipate being able to send him to school in the future. They thank the Lord in prayer.

As I read, the girls lean against me, Marilee's thick, honey-colored hair past her shoulders now, Penny's small, pale hand resting on my knee. William sets himself up on the floor, his arms and legs long and lanky like his father's. Their bodies stay quiet, riveted by this story from a time and place and life unlike our own.

We breathe a collective sigh when Billy wins the prize money and his grandfather survives the trip home. That night, the kids go to sleep with the satisfaction of a narrative that has involved hardship and perseverance and triumph in the end. The following evening, as the peepers begin their chorus outside and the evening sky turns black and cool, we read the final chapters.

Billy and the dogs go out hunting one more time. This night, a mountain lion prowls in the dark. The lion attacks. The dogs fight hard to protect Billy, and one of them, Old Dan, dies from his wounds. His sister, Little Ann, dies soon after. When we finish this chapter, William turns his face into his pillow, his back heaving as he tries to contain the emotion. I read the conclusion, in which the family moves to town and

Billy is able to go to school and his mother interprets the dogs' death as a sort of providential gift. When I close the book, William doesn't look at the rest of us. He pushes himself off the floor and retreats to his room. I tuck the girls in and then find him, still trembling, under his covers.

"I don't understand," he says. "It isn't a real story, so the author could have changed it. They didn't have to die."

I nod and rub his arm and say, "That's true. But even though it wasn't a real story, it was a true story about love between a boy and his dogs. Love always requires sacrifice."

"You love me," he says, "and that doesn't mean you have to die." He sounds defiant, as if he can argue me into a different ending.

"Right," I say. "But it means I would die if I needed to in order to protect you. And it means I make little sacrifices, like giving up sleep in the middle of the night or giving up time when you're sick and need to stay home from school. I give things up for you, even if I don't have to die because of it."

"But . . ." His voice trails off into a sigh and a shudder, as if he wants to keep up the protest, and yet he cannot summon the energy for it.

I sit with him until his breathing calms, and then I walk downstairs to close up the house for the night. As I lock the doors and turn off the lights in the playroom, my thoughts stay with love, with this concept that sounds so vague and emotional, this concept that works itself out through our bodies, through cups of cold water in the middle of the night and showing up for soccer games and cuddling on the couch and listening to their stories and praying for their futures.

My activities conclude in the kitchen, where I pull out turkey and ham and cheese for Marilee and William, pesto and mozzarella and tomato for Penny. The kids are old enough now to make their own lunches, but I like doing it for them. I enjoy the repetitive motion of spreading the mayonnaise, the knowledge that William likes three slices of ham and Penny prefers a roll to bread and Marilee wants her sandwich cut into triangles. As I tuck the food into plastic containers, I think about what love looks like when it isn't the love of a mother for her children or a boy for his dogs. It's natural for me to give of myself for our kids. Evolutionary biology alone explains how I am, by instinct as much as will, inclined to protect my offspring, my genetic inheritance. It is an act of self-preservation to love them as much as it is an act of self-sacrifice.

But I also believe that love is the only solution to the problems of our world that go beyond my immediate family and our little town. We are nearing the end of the presidential race between Hillary Clinton and Donald Trump. The rhetoric has become increasingly negative. Clinton is quoted as calling Trump supporters a "basket of deplorables." Trump is caught on tape joking about how he can grope women and forcibly kiss them. When I look at the divisions within our communities, divisions between ethnic groups and religious groups and economic groups and on down the line of vying social identities that this campaign has highlighted, I see love as the only way to bridge these divides, love as the only way to bring healing. But love can heal only if it is mutual. Love can heal only if it is offered freely, without condition, and then received and returned. The trust necessary for such an exchange of love is hard enough, but if love also requires sacrifice, who will make that sacrifice? Even if it is the right thing to do by some abstract ethical standard, why would anyone choose love over self if love means hardship, if love means pain?

I finish my tasks and get ready for bed, sliding under the covers and propping my elbows on my knees to read another chapter of an Ann Patchett novel. Soon I am blinking back sleep. I turn out the light and go through my bedtime ritual—check email one last time, scan the headlines, check the weather for tomorrow, text Peter good night. I set an alarm on my phone and turn on white noise, a signal to my brain that it is time to rest. But my mind stays active even as I curl up on my side and close my eyes.

I am thinking about sacrificial love that isn't directed toward family or close friends. I start with my parents, who keep in touch with Vera, who worked for us when we lived in Edenton. Mom and Dad provided Vera and her husband James with a low-interest loan a long time ago, giving them a way to own a house—a double-wide trailer in the country—even when they didn't have enough equity for a loan from the bank. I asked my dad about this arrangement once, and he shrugged. "I just have so much respect for them," he said.

"They tithe to their church no matter what amount of money they're making. They never missed a day of work." He didn't see the time or money he offered to them as a sacrifice. He saw it as respect. I am starting to see it as what it looks like to participate in the work of love.

I think about my friend Ginny, whose daughter Rachel has Down syndrome. Ginny is a white woman and a lawyer. Whether it comes as a result of wealth or education or career, the teachers, the special education director, and the principal of Rachel's school all listen to Ginny when she speaks on behalf of her child. Rachel has become friends with kids on the social margins of the school system in their town, kids with parents who didn't grow up speaking English and who don't have much money. As Ginny started advocating for change for Rachel, she realized Rachel's friends were not given the same treatment. She started advocating for those other kids as well. This work didn't emerge out of a sense of obligation to sacrifice her time or her social capital. It emerged out of reciprocal relationships of love.

I think of my friend Lisa, who has volunteered at a camp for kids who are growing up in a housing project in Philadelphia. Over the past few summers, Lisa and her kids have come to know and love one pair of brothers in particular. So when the boys' mom couldn't take care of them any longer and there wasn't any food in the house, they called Lisa. Lisa talked with her husband and kids, and they invited the brothers to come and stay for a while. It has been a sacrifice of time and money and emotion for the whole family, but not one that they regret making. The sacrifice was built with a foundation of love.

In our own household, our love for Penny has prompted us to connect with people outside our circle of friends and family. Over the years, we've shared meals and stories with couples who are expecting babies with Down syndrome. They've spanned racial and ethnic groups and had different levels of education and income. But it has felt natural to introduce them to Penny and follow up with emails and phone calls. We've hosted medical students who are trying to understand the social context of kids with disabilities. I'm not someone who typically spends time on the phone with strangers, but I will drop anything to talk with a woman who has recently received a prenatal diagnosis of Down syndrome. Looking in from the outside, these phone calls and emails and visits might look like sacrifice. We are giving of ourselves to people we otherwise never would have met. But it doesn't feel like sacrifice. It feels like what we want to do.

I think back to *Where the Red Fern Grows* and that conversation with William, and I realize that the dogs didn't fight the mountain lion out of an impulse toward self-sacrifice. Rather, they did so out of an instinct to love and protect this boy. Similarly, when Peter or I get up in the night because one of our kids needs us, or when I take an hour to tell a pregnant woman what it's like to have a child with Down syndrome, it isn't because we are aiming for sacrifice. It is simply the necessary action that grows out of love. Sacrifice emerges in response to the love that is already present. Sacrifice might be required, but not because sacrifice is the goal or the answer. Love is the goal. Love is the answer.

I am still thinking about the nature of love after I get the kids to school the next morning. I indulge my inner scholar and do an online word search. *Love* appears nearly seven hundred times in the Bible, twice as often as the word *pray*, and more than *faith* and *hope* combined. I look up a handful of these verses, and I return to the simple definition of God offered in the letter of First John: *God is love*. The passage where that description pops up is a swirling invitation to love, with love like a circle whose beginning and end cannot be identified precisely. The love of God spills out to creation, and once human beings receive that love, it spills out of us. I worry about whether or not I have it in me to love others sacrificially, but this passage reminds me that I don't need to generate love for others. I need to root my life in the source of the love that powers all of existence and let that love nourish me and grow me up. This passage in John's letter stands alongside the hundreds of other references to love throughout the books that make up the Bible, and together it is as if they are saying, *Let love consume your entire being. Let love be everything you are about. Let love define you, and everything else will follow.*

When I was in seminary, I learned about the concept of the Trinity, the Christian idea that God is one being in three persons—Father, Son, and Holy Spirit. If it's true that God exists in an ongoing and eternal relationship, as a being defined by everlasting and reciprocal and self-giving love, then love is the ground of all being, the ground of all existence. The more I situate myself in love, the more I situate myself in reality.

For most of the morning, I am uplifted by these lofty ideals, but doubt creeps in as the day wears on. Individual acts of love appear so small in the face of the world's needs. The examples I came up with the night before seem meager by the light of day. One family who could buy a trailer. A few kids who were treated fairly by a school system. Brothers who have a place to live. A handful of parents who chose to bring their children with Down syndrome into the world.

I once heard a story of a boy on a beach teeming with starfish, and the boy decided to pick one up and gently toss it back into the sea. It is a story that is supposed to demonstrate the power of an individual to make a real difference in the face of vast suffering. But the story quickly moves me to despair when I consider the thousands of starfish dying on the sand. I wonder whether acts of sacrificial love are like that boy on the beach, small ripples that do not come close to addressing the massive expanse of the need.

But maybe it is the story that's the problem. Vulnerable human beings are not starfish, incapable of advocating for themselves. And I am not a lone altruistic person on a beach full of helpless others. I am a similarly needy person looking for connection and meaning. And even the starfish are not stuck on the beach forever. The tide will rise. The water will wash over them and return them to the sea.

I have been thinking about love in terms of the capacity of individuals to give and sacrifice and care for others. But when Jesus talks about love, when Paul writes about love, they are addressing a whole group of people. "Y'all" would be a more accurate translation for almost every command in the Bible. The biblical writers are not calling *me* to love. They are calling *us*, together, to love. Martin Luther King Jr. and Gandhi and William Wilberforce and Elizabeth Cady Stanton were effective in enacting social change not because of their individual power but because of the collective work of thousands of people who stood with them in loving resistance to the status quo.

Love draws the vulnerable out of suffering and draws the powerful out of isolation. And yet our individual actions are drops in an ocean when entire systems and institutions perpetuate injustice and division. My correspondence with a young woman who is incarcerated due to a minor drug offense will not change the prison system. My friend who volunteers as a tutor in a local public school will not spark education reform. The money Peter and I give will help only a few kids in a limited way. Individuals loving other individuals—like my parents with Vera and James or Ginny with her daughter's friends or us with parents of children with Down syndrome—can make a meaningful difference in the lives of everyone involved, but they will not change the tide.

It makes me realize that while I want to be someone who loves others—and not only those within my own family and social network but also those outside my typical sphere—I also need to connect to others in order for the act of love to be transformative. I need to invest myself in and entrust myself to institutions—churches, schools, nonprofit organizations—that involve whole groups of people united by common concerns. Love by its nature is relational, and the power love wields is not through isolated individuals but through institutions and communities that band together on behalf of one another.

Our friends Brent and Elizabeth have recently received their second foster child after years of preparatory work. Kay is four years old, and she has been placed within a loving home with foster parents who can provide all the nurture and teaching and support a child could want. Kay cries every day for her mother, and Elizabeth longs for her foster daughter to be returned to her mom. Yet Kay's relationship with her mother has been jeopardized by this estrangement. Kay no longer wants to speak Spanish, and her mother has limited English. Elizabeth becomes more and more disillusioned with the system as she realizes that Kay cannot be reunited with her mother until her mother demonstrates housing stability, which is to say, until her mother makes more money, a near impossibility for a migrant worker. Elizabeth is powerless in the face of a system that seems bent on keeping this child from the one person she needs most in the world.

But my friend Sarah is involved in a church in Los Angeles where the entire church has committed itself to participating in the foster care system. There are 35,000 children in the foster system in Los Angeles. This church has thought through what it might mean for them to be involved corporately in loving these kids. It has partnered with the government to provide training for members, and it has formed community groups for support. Members of the church can sign up to become foster parents. Members can also become advocates for foster kids or identify themselves as support for a foster family. Not only does this create a web of support for the families but it also gets a whole disparate group of people involved in the system. So the lawyer who doesn't have time for a foster child nevertheless hears about the problems with the court system and starts to think about ways to advocate for change. Or the politician or the corporate executive or the teacher or whomever else might not ever welcome a child into their home now bumps up against the tangled knot of good intentions and bureaucracy and apathy and poverty and tragedy that leaves these kids on the margins. These individuals might begin to see ways to love kids in their own area of expertise. I can only imagine how love might change things when hundreds of people are connected and committed to care for the most vulnerable children in their city.

In Paul's letter to the church in Ephesus, he writes a lengthy prayer that is all about love. I've had that verse tacked to my wall for years, but I have only recently noticed the clause nestled right in the middle: "I pray that you, being rooted and established in love, may have power, together with all the Lord's holy people, to grasp how wide and long and high and deep is the love of Christ."[1] Paul prays for us to have power—together. God's love is something for us to know, for us to experience and live out of, together.

Love offers two invitations. One, for us to rest in the source of all love, to recognize that love does not originate within us but as a force that powers the universe and is freely and abundantly available to all who would receive it. And two, when we are living in and from that source of love, Love invites us to join with others who are living out of that same source, to make ourselves vulnerable together. It will require sacrifice. But we will not be thinking about the sacrifice. We will simply be allowing love to pour forth.

chapter thirteen

TO ACT JUSTLY

On the morning after Donald Trump's unexpected election as president of the United States, I get out of bed and work out and help the kids get ready for school. Penny and Marilee are disappointed to learn that a girl isn't going to be our next president. William is concerned that Trump hasn't really considered the cost of building a wall along the border with Mexico and that it will bankrupt our country. Peter is in Asia, with a twelve-hour time difference.

We drive to Marilee and William's Montessori school first, and I walk inside with all three kids. We have grown to love the rituals embedded in this place, with its celebrations of both religious holidays and moments like the winter solstice. We are grateful for its emphasis on traditional subjects like grammar and geography alongside its holistic approach to learning, with efforts like an outdoor classroom and teaching the children peaceful breathing as a way to combat stress. Usually, I am greeted by other moms and a few dads, all smiling, many wearing exercise clothes, with fresh muffins and coffee at the front door and teachers who welcome our children with a hug.

But this morning the adults are mostly silent, offering wry, toothless smiles as we pass. We approach William's classroom, where two mothers huddle against a bulletin board. One begins to cry. The other extends her arms. By the time Penny and I have dropped off Marilee, more women are crying, and the assistant head of school is shepherding them into the library and away from the children. A friend passes, squeezes my hand, and with a glance to Penny, whispers, "What happens when the rednecks decide who becomes president?"

For a moment I wonder if I could have heard her correctly—the scorn and fear and anger underneath her words. She waves and scoots into the library before I can decide how to respond. Penny and I walk out the door.

On our drive to school, Penny asks if we can play a word game where we choose a category and then the last letter of one word becomes the first letter of the next. We pick school: *music*, *cursive*, *English*, *homework* . . .

I pull up to Penny's drop-off. She shoulders her backpack and gives me a kiss on the cheek. As I move forward, a friend from church pulls her car close and rolls down her window. "I know he's not a role model for the kids," she says. "But

I'm relieved to hear the news this morning." Her eyes are soft. She—like my friend who is aghast by the "rednecks"—is looking for solidarity.

"It's definitely not what I expected we would wake up to," I say. I glance in my rearview mirror at the car behind me. My friend nods in recognition that I need to pull forward. She drives away.

A heaviness hangs over our community for the next few weeks. Most of the people I know are depressed by the election results. Others are happy but hesitant to express it. I am concerned about the way this election has drawn an invisible line within our community. Women are asking if I know who other women voted for. They aren't sure who they can be friends with anymore. I feel hollow inside—fearful in light of the new president's statements throughout his campaign about African Americans and Muslims and women and people with disabilities, and saddened by the animosity I hear toward people who voted for him. It is in the midst of all this angst that I am invited to pray.

Prayer is one of the few spiritual practices that is pointless unless God is real. Meditation calms the body whether or not there's a spiritual being receiving our deliberate breathing and clear mind. Reading sacred texts aligns us with the wisdom of our ancestors whether or not it was divinely inspired. Church attendance connects us to the needs of our community. Fasting cleanses the body of toxic substances. Resting on Sundays allows us to let go of stress and worry. But prayer? Taking time to pour out our needs and our anxieties, demanding change, confessing sin, crying out for help—all of these things depend upon the existence of God, and specifically the existence of a God who hears and responds to our cries. Prayer in the face of insurmountable problems is an admission of weakness and need. Prayer is a commitment to a better future, a sign of faith that the world will one day be made right. Prayer is an act that emerges out of helplessness. Prayer is an act of hope.

As a white person who is also an oldest child with a type A personality, I tend to think that problems can be solved as long as we put enough work into their solutions. But after years of thinking about the problems of racial injustice and economic inequality and discrimination against kids and adults with disabilities, I have finally conceded that these social ills will not be overcome by individual goodwill or smarter policies or tweaks in the system.

Even secular writers often use a spiritual word, *sin*, to describe the injustice of racism. Sin is a word that encompasses both individual wrongdoing and broader denial of equality and opportunity. And as much as I believe that policies can change systems of injustice, and as much as I believe that individuals can be empowered to make positive choices, I am starting to believe that the most powerful way to combat sin is spiritual at its core. Yes, the answer to sin is love, but the way to tap into that love is through prayer. Prayer is not a way to avoid action, but it is an acknowledgment of the futility of action without God's help.

The first invitation to pray arrives via email from a friend in California who feels saddened by her friends and family members who will not talk to one another based upon their divergent votes. She suggests that we can join our religious forebears and choose a time for prayer and fasting. Like the calls from the prophets of old, she invites people of faith on both sides of the voting aisle to commit ourselves to a spiritual purpose that transcends politics. She suggests we take the time we would typically spend eating one meal and instead give that time to prayer. She invites Trump voters and Clinton voters and suggests the Lord's Prayer as a guide to invite God's will, God's Kingdom, and God's healing into our national divisions. I sign myself up immediately. Within a few weeks, another friend sends an email inviting me to join a separate chain of prayer for justice, mercy, and healing in our land. In this case, the invitation goes out to Muslims, agnostics, Christians, and Jews—again, to people who are divided by politics but united by a desire to see healing.

I agree to pray from 12 to 12:30 on Mondays, and I begin fasting from lunch on that day. At first, it is exhilarating. Every time I feel a pang of hunger, I remind myself that I hunger for justice. Every time my eyes wander toward the refrigerator, I offer up a prayer for one of the families whose loved ones have been shot by police, or I pray for President Trump and his team to do justice as they set policy, or I pray for victims of various crimes to receive healing. I daydream about starting a blog that would curate these prayers and stories and ideas about how to become more politically and personally engaged on these issues. I start reading more about our criminal justice system, the foster care system, the refugee crisis.

After about two months, the shine starts to fade. The political landscape isn't any different than it was before. The social problems remain. There are still news reports of police shootings of unarmed black men and deportations of undocumented immigrants who have been separated from their children. Stories closer to home underscore the slowly unfolding tragedy of despair in various white communities: A friend calls to tell me her husband is addicted to painkillers, and she is seeking a divorce. An old classmate dies from a heroin overdose. I find myself fretting in my minivan, coming up with all sorts of ideas for how I might help enact change, but those ideas never become actions in the face of the time spent caring for our family and household and continuing the teaching and writing I am already doing.

Not only that, but sitting still and praying about one topic for thirty minutes, while hungry, gets harder every week. I try to remind myself of the millions of people in the world who go without lunch involuntarily. I try to make a mental connection between the hunger I feel for a sandwich and the hunger I want to feel for things to be made right. But mostly I feel grumpy and distracted. My thoughts turn with almost a shrug toward the possibility that at least I might lose weight with this new practice.

But at the same time, there come little whispers, sentences that hang like threads of truth that I would miss unless I pay attention. *How long do you think your African American brothers and sisters have been praying for justice? How many prayers have seemed unanswered for them? How many places in the Bible do people cry out, asking, "How long, O Lord"? Are you willing to join this work of prayer no matter what the outcome, no matter how long it takes, no matter how many meals you miss or how futile the time seems?*

How easy it is for me to slip into a mentality of power, believing that all will magically and quickly be well because finally I have woken up and responded to wrongs that have been going on for generations.

In the midst of my spiritual weariness, a friend from church mentions that he—a white man with a handlebar mustache and a penchant for Tae Kwon Do—has been listening to African American spirituals lately. He doesn't know anything about my recent practice of prayer, but he says, "I got kind of annoyed." He looks down, almost apologetic, and then continues, "The music was beautiful, but at the same time it just kept going on and on and on, especially the part that was sad. It was like the sadness was never going to end, but they were going to keep singing about it until they got an answer."

His experience of listening echoes my experience of prayer. His words come as a strange affirmation that we are invited to cry out until things change for good, and when they don't change, to persevere in faith, not by pretending it's all better but by continuing to cry out.

And even though I question my commitment to this effort, and even though it feels futile and frustrating and I want to give up, I also start to see shoots of growth. First, in my own thinking. As I pray through the Lord's Prayer with justice in mind, I am struck by that very basic sentence, "Give us this day our daily bread."[1] What pops out at me is the corporate nature of those words. It isn't "Give *me* this day *my* daily bread" or "Give *my* family our daily bread," though in the past that has been how I was inclined to think about that clause. I used to even translate that line in the prayer into the specifics of my daily life: *Give me what I need to take care of these children. Give me the words I need to write. Give me what I need to get through another day of managing our household.* Give me.

But Jesus instructs us to pray very differently. His prayer includes me, but it is so much bigger than me. Give us. All of us. I'm not just praying for what I need. My relationship with God isn't just about me and my family. It's about entering into the needs of others and imploring for all of us. I see my own self-centeredness that day. I see that my reluctance in prayer isn't just about boredom or hunger or futility; it is also about my own unwillingness to acknowledge and respond to the needs of my brothers and sisters in this world.

Another Monday, when I am daydreaming about the food I'm not eating and my mind is wandering away from the praying I am supposed to be doing, I try to focus my attention by reading a series of verses from the Psalms and the Prophets about justice. I find a sampling:

> Administer true justice; show mercy and compassion to one another.[2]

The LORD loves righteousness and justice;
the earth is full of his unfailing love.[3]

The LORD longs to be gracious to you;
therefore he will rise up to show you compassion.
For the LORD is a God of justice.[4]

When I read those words, instead of guiding my prayers, they help me realize how little I understand the biblical notion of justice. I typically think of justice as making sure that when people do things that are wrong, they get the punishment they deserve. But here, God's justice is not focused on punishing the wrongdoer. Rather, it is focused on protecting the vulnerable and restoring peace. Justice has to do with restoring relationships, with healing the social and emotional and spiritual fabric of individual lives and whole communities. God's justice isn't really about who should go to jail and who should be compensated for wrongdoing. It is about a whole different way of being in the world—God's way of being in the world, with mercy and unfailing love and compassion at the center.

In the midst of these meager attempts at prayer, I start to see myself differently. With my Princeton degree and my experiences as someone who can argue a case and get what I want, I have been seeing the problems of racism and class divides in our country through the lens of superiority. I think I have the things that everyone else wants, and now I am enlightened enough to share. *Here, have my education and my way of dressing and my reserved emotions and my exercise regime. Have my positive discipline methods for your children. Have my wealth so that your daughter can go to ballet class and your son can take piano lessons. Have my walks through the woods and my sweet little town with the green and the churches and the white picket fences.* It strikes me that there are plenty of people who don't want ballet class and the New England countryside. But they do want to be treated with dignity. They do want fairness. They do want safety and stability and opportunity. My life is not the answer to the world's problems, and it humbles me to see the ways I have assumed that it is.

One other verse strikes me almost like a blow. It comes from Micah, one of the short, prophetic books in the Bible. When I was younger, I learned a song set to these words, so they have been inscribed on my consciousness for decades. But today, as I look at the passage again, I see something I have never seen before. Micah 6:8 reads,

> He has shown you, O mortal, what is good.
> And what does the LORD require of you?
> To act justly and to love mercy
> and to walk humbly with your God.

For many years, I have been someone who wanted to act justly and love mercy, but finally I see how often I have done so without any humility, without any acknowledgment of my own inadequacy, my own helplessness, my own need. For so long, I have wanted to change the rest of the world. I didn't want the rest of the world to change me.

But this practice of prayer is changing me. I thought it would bring me face to face with the pain of the world outside. Instead, it is making me aware of the ways I cut myself off from that pain through alcohol, entertainment, judgment, or other distractions. I thought prayer would show me how I could take action. Instead, it is beginning to show me how much I still need to learn.

Weeks pass. I fast somewhat halfheartedly, and sometimes I fall asleep on my desk while praying, and prayer does not open up a miraculous way for me to move beyond the walls of my privilege. I feel helpless. I feel as though my prayer will never amount to anything.

But then God gives me a glimpse of what the future might hold, what might happen in me, in others, if we are willing to watch and pray.

It is a Monday, but I am neither fasting nor praying because I am speaking at a church in Greenwich, Connecticut. The room is full of women who in many ways are like me—white, affluent, educated, religious. And today one of my mom's good friends from my hometown, Edenton, is in the room. Her daughter now lives in Greenwich, and she has come up to visit. After I finish speaking, we embrace. Missie doesn't let go of my hand, and although I am a forty-year-old woman, a part of me feels like a little girl again. When I was a child, I spent the night in her house regularly. She taught me how to draw. She was my Vacation Bible School teacher.

She led us in making T-shirts of the fruit of the Spirit, with colorful painted stamps of grapes and apples and oranges to remind us of love and joy and peace.

She asks what I'm working on, and when I tell her I am finishing up a book about privilege, she says, "Oh, I have so much to tell you."

I say, "I would love to hear more."

"Well, Amy Julia," she says, "there's violence in Edenton now. And a boy I knew—a young black man—was shot. It was an accident, not intentional, but it just ate me up. His grandma was our church secretary, and I knew that boy. I knew him and then he was gone and I was so sad and so"—she inhaled deeply—"just so angry. I was walking around in all this anger for a few days."

Missie is one of the smallest people I know, but her petite frame emanates strength. She doesn't speak with the drawl I remember from my childhood, but her words have more warmth and richness than our flat Connecticut accents. I am riveted by her story.

She says, "So then I was pushing my grandson on the swing at the playground, and I was next to Tonia. Now I don't know Tonia, but we introduced ourselves and got to talking about the violence in town. Edenton's still as small as it was when you lived there. Tonia is black and of course she knew this boy who died. I just kept saying, 'What are we going to do? What are we going to do?'

"The next day I got a letter. It was from Tonia. And it said, 'Here's what you can do.' It was a list of things like calling the chief of police and working for school reform and all these initiatives."

There are fifty other women in the room, but I am fixed on Missie and her words. I laugh when she tells me about the letter. I can only imagine the surprise she felt when she received it.

She nods. "Yep. So you know what I did with that letter? I put it at the bottom of a pile at my desk. I had been saying I wanted something to do, but I didn't really. I just wanted to pray about it and not know what to do and go on the same way."

I nod now, thinking of my own reticence to get involved, my own excuses. I say, "I've told Peter before that I'm too polite to be an activist. I understand."

"Well, after a few weeks, I couldn't let it sit there anymore. So I dug that letter out of the papers on my desk and I called the chief of police and I told him I was so upset about this violence in our community and he said, 'Mothers Against Violence. That's exactly what I need.' So I guess I'm an activist now. We have three different branches—there's a school-reform piece, and a reentry ministry for people who are coming out of prison, and then there's the prayer piece. That's what I'm in charge of."

She stops and glances around and says, "I should let you talk to other people."

I shake my head and say, "That's okay. What does the prayer piece look like?"

She smiles. "It looks like me and several local pastors and

several town officials and a handful of other white and black folks gathering every time there's an act of violence in our community. We go to that place, and we hold hands in a circle, and we pray. We also gather once a month to pray for peace and unity and restoration."

We are still holding hands. I want to hear stories about my hometown for another hour. But Missie has a flight to catch, and I should speak with other people in the room. I am left with an image of this woman, whose great-great-grandfather owned slaves, standing alongside her African American brothers and sisters, all the Lord's holy people praying, together, for their town.

And it strikes me that this is where healing could happen, this is where love could pour forth, this is where centuries of hurt could start to mend.

I have not been given a list of things to do in response to the hurt in our world. But for months and perhaps years to come, I will join with others in praying and fasting for justice on Mondays, not because I believe our prayers will exert control over God's work but because I believe our prayers are a part of God's work. And as meager and ineffective as my prayer is, it nevertheless keeps me tethered to hope. Prayer is not a guarantee. It is an act of faith that God is love, that I am needy, and that by turning toward love, I will someday, somehow be given a way to participate in the restoration of the good world God made.

chapter fourteen

A REVERSAL

"Do you want to get well?"

Jesus asks this question of a man who has been "an invalid" for thirty-eight years. The man is lying near a pool of water that is said to contain healing power, so the answer to the question seems obvious. The man cannot walk. He is near a potential source of healing. Of course he wants to get well.

But the man doesn't answer Jesus' question. Instead, he gives a reason why he isn't already well. "I have no one to help me into the pool when the water is stirred," he says.

Jesus, who already knows who this man is and how long he has been in this condition, doesn't repeat himself. He issues a command: "Get up! Pick up your mat and walk." And then,

John writes, "At once the man was cured; he picked up his mat and walked."[1]

Do you want to get well? It seems like a question with a clear answer, but I can relate to that man lying by the water, making weak and ineffectual attempts to cure myself. When I was sick in high school, did I want to get well? When I was angry at our children and at my husband and at God and I was eating and drinking too much, did I want to get well? And now, as I confront the harm to me, to my friends and family, and to countless others by a social structure that has been built on exclusion, do I want to get well?

Do we want to get well?

When I was in my early twenties, Peter and I were both working with high-school kids, and a generous and wealthy woman decided to send us and a dozen other youth ministers to a monastic community in the Burgundy region of France. We happily accepted the trip. Before we left the US, I noticed a twinge of pain in my lower jaw, as if I had bruised it by chewing too hard. It still hurt after a few days of only chewing on the other side of my mouth, but I didn't have time to go to the dentist, so I told myself it would get better on its own.

By the time we reached the monastery two days later, my jaw was throbbing. It was all I could think about. On the fourth night of our stay, my mouth pulsed with pain. I tried to ease it with three glasses of wine, a Percocet that one of our companions had packed in case of emergency, and two Tylenol PM. Nothing helped. Lying in bed that night,

I grimaced and curled up in a ball and hit other parts of my body to try to distract myself from how much it hurt.

Peter drove me to a dentist in the morning. Our French was limited. Peter said to the dentist, "*Mal à la dent,*" and the dentist replied, "We pull za tooth!" I sat propped up on an examination table watching their exchange. "*Non!* We do not pull za tooth!" Peter said, speaking English with a French accent. I breathed as slowly and deeply as I could.

The dentist agreed not to pull my tooth. Instead he took a scalpel and—without administering Novocain—sliced open my gum. Sweat began to pop off my body. I gripped Peter's hand. My eyes were closed, but Peter says my skin turned green as he watched the dentist dig black gunk out of my mouth. The relief was immediate. We paid twenty-seven euros and walked away with a bottle of antibiotics and some Advil.

At first, I hadn't wanted to get well because I didn't have time. Healing was inconvenient. I was able to ignore the problem. As the pain intensified, I denied the truth of the situation and tried to cure myself with a dangerous combination of substances. The final cure—which needed to come from an external, more knowledgeable source—was excruciating. My body responded with violent protest. And then the healing could begin.

I look at the history of harm in our nation—from the eradication of the Native American population and the transatlantic slave trade, to Jim Crow laws and eugenics and institutionalization for people with intellectual disabilities, evolving to our current moment of mass incarceration and income inequality and injustices throughout the immigration system and an opioid epidemic and anxiety and depression and despair—and I wonder, *Do we want to get well?*

In one article about the historic inequities within governmental housing policies, Ta-Nehisi Coates, a national correspondent for *The Atlantic*, calls for a "national reckoning" with this history of injustice, a reckoning that "would lead to spiritual renewal."[2] Since Coates describes himself as an atheist, I assume he doesn't take the ancient Creation stories of Genesis as his guide in spiritual matters. But like many Christians, Coates identifies this historic injustice as a spiritual problem, and when I think about the roots of spiritual harm, I go back to the Garden, back to Eden. I think about the curses God proclaims upon Adam and Eve when they refuse to acknowledge God as the one who will guide them, when they start pointing fingers at one another and shifting blame, when they turn in upon themselves. I look at the problems in our contemporary moment that mirror that episode way back when, pitting the police against the community, the rich against the poor, the conservatives against the liberals, the evangelicals against the atheists. Adam and Eve chose self over relationship, preservation over surrender, fear over love. Humans throughout history have followed their lead. The only way out is a reversal. And the only hope for a reversal is a reversal powered by Love.

I spent years observing the privilege of my life, first as a child who knew that there was something wrong with race-based de facto segregation in schools and churches and job opportunities, later as a student who learned the history and the terminology for systems of oppression. The injustice of our world saddened me, and I made meager attempts to participate in its undoing. But it wasn't until I had a child who straddled the world of privilege and the world of exclusion that I began to see my own complicity in the systems I had for so long critiqued from a distance.

I began to see that my admission to Princeton wasn't just about hard work. I began to see that my marriage and our careers weren't just about answered prayer. I began to see my own participation in the harmful policies that still excluded many people of color and many people without significant financial means from home ownership, from living in good school districts, from consideration for jobs. And I began to see that this life of privilege didn't simply harm the people cut off from it, but harmed those of us within it as well, as we found ourselves caught in a cycle of anxiety and depression and homogeneity that failed to call forth the rich, complicated, messy, beautiful depths of our humanity.

I now understand two things about privilege that I didn't understand before. One, that privilege in and of itself is not a sign of God's blessing but rather a fact of my life that can be used for good or for ill. Two, that what our culture calls privilege is a mirage, a false understanding of what it means to live a good life, and that the true privilege of my existence comes in the undeserved favor I have in being one who is loved by God, loved by others, and able to love in return.

But for me to be able to live in love, I have to come face to face with sin, with everything that separates me from love. When I reckon with both sin and love, I am prompted to confess, an act that has two distinct meanings. To confess is to admit guilt, but it is also to acknowledge truth. Christians confess their sins before a priest or in private prayer. Christians also confess their faith, whether in informal proclamations or in formal statements such as the Westminster Confession. St. Augustine's classic spiritual memoir *Confessions* is itself both a confession of guilt and a confession of faith. And whether confessing sin or confessing faith, the act of confession initiates a process of transformation, restoration, and healing. Both confessions of faith and confessions of guilt can leave us immobile, vulnerable, humbled. And both confessions of guilt and confessions of faith require acknowledgment of a power greater than ourselves.

This book is an attempt at both a confession of sin and a confession of faith—faith not in privilege, but faith in the God of love who invites me to understand privilege differently.

I acknowledge my privilege, which in and of itself brings an awareness of the damage it has done as well as the gifts it has given me. I also confess my privilege—that I am guilty of unwillingness to sacrifice for the good of others, and I am guilty of judgment and ignorance and apathy toward others. I am guilty of not loving my neighbors. My confession is also an admission that, on my own, I am powerless to heal the wounds these decisions have inflicted upon my own psyche and the wounds they have inflicted upon others.

One of the gifts of confessing sins to God is the thought that we do not have to carry those sins anymore. Rather, we take the burden of guilt and offer it to God. In return, God offers healing. I bring my junk; God gives me riches. It's a remarkable exchange.

This healing isn't offered because God minimizes the seriousness of sin, and it isn't offered because God doesn't care about the people my sin has harmed. We deface the image of God every time we disdain or abuse another human being. But if sin is like punching someone in the face, then confession is realizing that the person I punched is related to a doctor, and asking the doctor to bandage up my wounded knuckles. God is the doctor who agrees to bandage those wounds. We confess to God and receive healing from God, but God's work in us is not finished until we also confess and work toward healing in and for the people we have harmed. In fact, if confession is in some sense a plea for healing, it is a plea for healing that enables us to move toward a larger work of love.

As I was working on the conclusion for this book, I tried to come up with action steps that individuals or communities could take in response to privilege. I tried to write inspirational stories. I even thought about throwing myself into a social justice initiative simply to have a personal anecdote of redemption in these pages. Instead, I find myself chastened and humbled, powerless and vulnerable, waiting with hope that I will be shown a way toward healing. The story of privilege in America, and the story of privilege in my own life, has not come to a satisfying conclusion.

But this story has come to a beginning. Bryan Stevenson, author of *Just Mercy* and a lawyer who defends African American men serving life sentences or facing the death penalty, said in an interview, "We [as Christians] have an insight on what is on the other side of repentance, what is on the other side of acknowledgement of wrongdoing—which is repair."[3]

Confession is a small offering. And yet it is also the foundation of repair. I am one vulnerable, distractible, self-centered human being trying to come to terms with the gifts and sorrows of my life. It will take thousands upon thousands of others who are willing to do the same, to bow our knees and take up a posture of humility, of listening to others instead of insisting on hearing our own voices, of admitting our own complicity in harm, of opening our hands and hearts to healing even when it hurts.

Confession is not the end of the story, but it is a position from which people of privilege can lay down the burden of the sin of exclusion, a position from which people of privilege can ask for help in knowing what to do next, a position from which the wounded—both the victims and the perpetrators—can acknowledge their need to get well.

Jesus calls on people to confess their sins when he says, "Repent, for the kingdom of heaven has come near" (Matthew 4:17). At its root, *repent* means to turn around—to confess that you are headed in the wrong direction, and then to turn your back on that erroneous path and head the other way. For Jesus, confession is only the beginning, the first crucial step on a new journey, a new vista, a new way of being.

But Jesus' call to repentance is not the center of his message. Rather, it is a necessary preliminary action that leads to the most important pronouncement: "The kingdom of heaven has come near." Jesus proclaims God's Kingdom—a place where love reigns, where the different peoples and nations of the earth live in love with one another, a place where there is justice and mercy and healing and freedom. And repentance—turning away from self, away from anxiety, away from exclusion—is the way to enter that wholeness.

Repentance is not about feeling terrible for wrongdoing, but about turning away from everything—including wrongdoing—that prevents us from seeing and participating in the good work that God is about. Repentance is an invitation to fullness of life, to a connected life, to a life of hope. When we turn away from ourselves—away from the allure of tribalism, away from the temptation of self-justification—and turn toward Love, we begin to construct a vision of the future formed and shaped by hope, by the possibilities of unexpected connections, of mutual blessing, of a world made right.

Do we want to get well?

Acknowledgments

I started writing this book years ago, and for a long time I thought it was a book about reading out loud to our children. During a weeklong writer's workshop at the Collegeville Institute in Minnesota with Lauren Winner, I began to write about my own childhood, and I started to get a sense that this book was about more than books. Rachel Marie Stone and Katherine Willis Pershey were two of my companions that week, and their comments and encouragement, alongside Lauren's encouragement, helped me explore the ways children's books had been both a bridge and a wall in my understanding of identity and the world. Thank you.

Meanwhile, my agent, Chris Park, kept telling me that the "book book" wasn't quite working, and then a conversation with Carey Wallace helped me recognize that I was circling around the topic of privilege without even knowing it. I am thankful for these women and their patience and perseverance in getting me to this place, as well as for the women of INK and OKJFC who helped me come up with the title and helped me navigate some of the tricky waters of writing it.

Patricia Clarke read and critiqued multiple drafts and has

prayed for this book from its inception. Patricia Raybon similarly read and critiqued multiple drafts with honesty and graciousness and both personal and editorial wisdom. My friends Jennifer Grant, Niroshini Feliciano, Marlena Graves, Eliza Paolucci, Tal Fagin, Corey Widmer, Kelley Nicholson-Flynn, George Estreich, Andy Crouch, Sharon Hodde Miller, my sister Brooks Truesdell, and my parents all provided comments on early versions of the book that helped it reach its final shape. Jaclyn Grasso, my writing assistant, has championed this book from behind the scenes, fielded research questions, and even tracked down an outdated textbook from the 1980s with grace and good humor. I am grateful for the time all these people offered me and for their individual and collective wisdom.

Don Pape, Dave Zimmerman, and the team at NavPress have seen the possibilities for this book from the beginning. Dave, your encouragement and insight pushed me to rewrite whole chapters and made this book better than it ever could have been otherwise. Elizabeth Symm, your thoughtful attention to detail made every page better. Thank you.

Finally, I'm thankful for my family. For our kids, who occasionally checked in about the progress of the book but more often gave me reasons to leave it behind and remember the simple joys of life when I'm not living inside my own head. And for Peter, who sat through countless dinner conversations about memory and childhood and wealth and opportunity and love and healing and all the rest. It always feels inadequate to try to put it into words, but the least I can do is say thank you.

Questions for Discussion

1. The author shares about the "flinching" she experienced as she set out to write this book. What internal tension or resistance did you notice in yourself as you began reading? What tension do you feel as you enter into this discussion of privilege?

2. What was your exposure to the concept of social, economic, racial, or other kinds of privilege prior to reading this book? What were your impressions of privilege as a factor in society?

3. The idea that "life is a gift" seems uncontroversial. But consider the responses the author heard to her article about having Penny, her daughter with Down syndrome: "Many people criticized my decision. They even chastised me for . . . the suffering the condition would bring to the child, the burden it would place on the child's family, and the cost society would have to

bear" (page 10). What responsibilities come to us, as individuals and as a community, when we assert that every life is indeed a gift?

4. Think back on the stories you read and heard as a child. How, if at all, were people of different ethnicities and national backgrounds represented? What mental images do you have from those stories? The idea of representation—the possibility for people of different ethnicities and abilities to see people like them in film, literature, and other media—is growing in importance for people working in the arts. Why might it be important for people to see their lives represented in the stories they see, hear, and read? Why might it be important for people to see people unlike themselves represented in the arts?

5. "Mine was a happy childhood" (page 32). How would you characterize your childhood, generally speaking? Thinking back, what social inequities and discord do you suspect you were protected from as a child? In what ways might your upbringing have "limited and constrained" (page 36) your perception of what constituted a normal life? What opportunities might you have missed?

6. What do you wish you'd been protected from? What hardships and discomforts did you experience that in

adulthood you've discovered were not experienced by other people—especially people who are of a different ethnicity or socioeconomic background than yours?

7. Think about the story of the place where you grew up. What do you know about its history as it relates to race? What about the place where you grew up do you suspect might be different from what you assumed about it (or were taught about it) when you were young?

8. The author mentions "linguistic whitewashing" (page 44) as a means of "painting over the ugly truth" of such things as the slave trade and Native American displacement in US history. Where do you observe "linguistic whitewashing" in discussion of sensitive cultural issues? Why do you think so many people gravitate toward "safe," "tame," or "politically correct" language when it comes to difficult topics? In what ways can carefully considered language make dialogue about difficult issues more constructive? What are the problems and possibilities for politically correct language?

9. The author's story involves growing up in the American South (known for its complicated racial history) and also living in the North Atlantic (sometimes presumed to be free of racial tension). What surprised you about

her descriptions, as they pertain to racial tension, of North Carolina? Of Connecticut?

10. The author writes about her reaction to the news of the death of Philando Castile after being shot by a police officer during a routine traffic stop. Do you recall hearing reports of that story? Maybe there's another, similar story of a person of color dying during an encounter with police that comes more quickly to mind for you (the author mentions Michael Brown, Eric Garner, Freddie Gray, Sandra Bland, and Tamir Rice). What do you remember about your reaction to the news report? What emotions do you recall experiencing? What do you suppose was driving those emotions for you?

11. "On the one hand, affluence seems to make relationships easier. . . . And yet, our affluence also fences us off from other people" (page 91). Conversations about social privilege often emphasize the unearned benefits of socioeconomic class or race or ability, but as you reflect on your background, do you see any challenges associated with privilege?

12. "I imagine Jesus . . . saying, *You don't need to worry about social status. You don't need to bow down to the god of career success. You don't need to become an expert parent*" (page 96). In what ways might unearned social

privilege be a burden God wants to relieve us of? In what ways might confronting our own unearned privilege be considered an act of faith?

13. "Told one way, it is a miracle that I met my husband" (page 105). What examples of "miracles" can you point to in your life that, on reflection, might be the result of circumstances related to your social status, ethnicity, and so on? What difference would it make to your story to consider the "alternative reading of the events" (page 111)?

14. "Privilege means being given a special status . . . being undeservedly yet unquestionably singled out" (page 129). Understood in this way, how might your experience of privilege be considered a matter of stewardship? What responsibilities might be associated with the privilege you've identified in your life?

15. "For all the ways in which Penny can identify as a person of privilege, she is also aligned with people who have been marginalized and oppressed through the centuries" (page 137). The author here acknowledges a basic *intersectionality*—the convergence of categories and classifications, such as ethnicity and gender and ability, that we observe in ourselves or have imposed on us. What intersectionality can you observe in your own life? How might that intersectionality help you more

fully empathize with people of different backgrounds than yourself?

16. "*Why is difference scary?*" (page 139). What causes people to focus on the differences they observe between themselves and other people? What value do you see in looking first for commonalities? How is this different from being "blind" to color or disability or other differences?

17. "Your value—like Penny's, like mine—comes because you are known and you are loved" (page 153). Does this assertion resonate for you? In what way is this assurance freeing for people of relative privilege? How might it be freeing for people who have not benefited as much from unearned privilege?

18. The author tells stories about physical healing at various points throughout the narrative. She writes, "I have come to believe that privilege harms everyone, those who are excluded from it and those who benefit from it" (page xxiv). In what ways does privilege harm people? How does the experience of physical harm and healing help us consider ways forward for healing the wounds inflicted by privilege?

19. In considering how we might participate in healing, the author writes, "Perhaps sharing our stories is a

beginning" (page 79). How do books and stories hinder or promote healing in this narrative? How would sharing our stories help foster connection or increase division?

20. What is the relationship between prayer and action? Is the author's call to prayer a passive response, a way out of responsibility? In what ways might prayer be considered a responsible act, even a catalytic act?

21. "When I reckon with both sin and love, I am prompted to confess" (page 190). What has this book helped you to identify in your life and your community in relation to the idea of unearned social privilege? What has been especially difficult for you to consider as you've read the book? What opportunities for transformation—personal, relational, societal—have come into view for you as you've considered the concept of privilege?

22. "For Jesus, confession is only the beginning, the first crucial step on a new journey" (page 192). What next steps have come into view for you as you've wrestled through this book with the concept of privilege? What possibilities open up for you personally, relationally, and as part of a community as you consider the influence of privilege on your life?

Notes

Foreword: Strangers at the Gate

1. Jeffrey Santa Ana, "Feeling in Radical Consciousness: James Baldwin's Anger as a Critique of Capitalism," in *James Baldwin: Challenging Authors*, ed. A. Scott Henderson and P. L. Thomas (Rotterdam: Sense Publishers, 2014), 91.
2. George Orwell, "Why I Write," in *A Collection of Essays* (Orlando: Harcourt, 1981), 315.
3. Joshua Rothman, "The Origins of 'Privilege,'" *New Yorker*, May 12, 2014, https://www.newyorker.com/books/page-turner/the-origins-of-privilege.
4. Peggy McIntosh, "White Privilege and Male Privilege: A Personal Account of Coming to See Correspondences through Work in Women's Studies," Working Paper No. 189 (Wellesley, MA: Wellesley Centers for Women, The National Seed Project, 1988), http://www.collegeart.org/pdf/diversity/white-privilege-and-male-privilege.pdf. See also https://nationalseedproject.org/white-privilege-unpacking-the-invisible-knapsack.
5. McIntosh, "White Privilege."
6. Richard J. Foster, *Celebration of Discipline: The Path to Spiritual Growth* (San Francisco, CA: HarperSanFrancisco, 1988), 10.

Chapter 1: Life Is a Gift

1. Elisa wrote about her daughter Eden for my blog. See Elisa Fryling Stanford, "What Slowing Down Teaches You That Rushing Never Will," *Thin Places* (blog), *Christianity Today*, April 29, 2014, http://www.christianitytoday.com/amyjuliabecker/2014/april/what-slowing-down-teaches-you-that-rushing-never-will.html.

Chapter 2: Mirrors and Doors

1. For more on the complicated issue of race and ethnicity in children's literature, read Christopher Myers's "The Apartheid of Children's Literature," *New York Times*, March 15, 2014, https://www.nytimes.com/2014/03/16/opinion/sunday/the-apartheid-of-childrens-literature.html and "Kwame Alexander on Children's Books and the Color of Characters," *New York Times*, August 26, 2016, https://www.nytimes.com/2016/08/28/books/review/kwame-alexander-on-childrens-books-and-the-color-of-characters.html?_r=0.
2. "Publishing Statistics on Children's Books about People of Color and First/Native Nations and by People of Color and First/Native Nations Authors and Illustrators," Cooperative Children's Book Center, accessed February 2, 2018, http://ccbc.education.wisc.edu/books/pcstats.asp.
3. Toni Morrison, *Playing in the Dark: Whiteness and the Literary Imagination* (reprint, New York, NY: Vintage Books, 1993), chapter 1, https://books.google.com/books?id=2dVas48cQNgC&printsec=frontcover&dq=playing+in+the+dark+whiteness+and+the+literary+imagination&hl=en&sa=X&ved=0ahUKEwjJzZ7ltZLaAhUsyoMKHYSCCQwQ6AEIJzAA#v=onepage&q=american%20africanism&f=false.
4. Toni Morrison, *Playing in the Dark*, 52.
5. For more about the racialized history of the Oompa Loompas, go to: Chryl Corbin, "Deconstructing Willy Wonka's Chocolate Factory: Race, Labor, and the Changing Depictions of the Oompa-Loompas," *Berkeley McNair Research Journal* 19 (Spring 2012): 47–63, http://ourenvironment.berkeley.edu/wp-content/uploads/2012/07/UCB_McNair_Journal_2012_wc.pdf.
6. For more about the racialized nature of the Calormen, see Taylor Marvin, "Assimilating into Narnian Whiteness, or Else," *Smoke and Stir*, May 15, 2014, https://smokeandstir.org/2014/05/15/assimilating-into-narnian-whiteness-or-else/.
7. "Award-Winners," *Reading Rockets*, WETA, accessed February 16, 2018, http://www.readingrockets.org/books/awardwinners#king.
8. Laura Ingalls Wilder, *The Long Winter* (reprint, New York, NY: HarperCollins, 2008), 122.

Chapter 4: A History of Cancer

1. W. Frank Ainsley, *North Carolina, the Land and Its People* (Atlanta, GA: Silver Burdett & Ginn, 1988), 88.
2. Ainsley, *North Carolina*, 93.
3. Ainsley, *North Carolina*, 102.

4. Ainsley, *North Carolina*, 168.
5. Isabel Wilkerson, "The Heart Is the Last Frontier," Interview with Krista Tippett, *On Being*, November 17. 2016, https://onbeing.org/programs/isabel-wilkerson-the-heart-is-the-last-frontier-nov2016/.
6. To learn more about the history of race in American schools, see "A History of Private Schools & Race in the American South," Southern Education Foundation, accessed April 2, 2018, http://www.southerneducation.org/Our-Strategies/Research-and-Publications/Race-Ethnicity-Landing-Pages/A-History-of-Private-Schools-Race-in-the-American.aspx.

Chapter 5: Banal Evils

1. A fascinating oral history with Dr. Slade and his wife is available here: http://docsouth.unc.edu/sohp/html_use/R-0019.html.
2. John G. Zehmer Jr., *Hayes: The Plantation, Its People, and Their Papers* (Raleigh, NC: North Carolina Office of Archives and History, 2007), 75.
3. Robert Hanna, Max Marchitello, and Catherine Brown, "Comparable but Unequal: School Funding Disparities," Connecticut School Finance Project, March 2015, http://ctschoolfinance.org/assets/uploads/files/Comparable-but-Unequal—School-Funding-Disparities.pdf.
4. Lincoln Caplan, "Two Connecticut School Systems, for the Rich and Poor," *New Yorker*, September 14, 2016, https://www.newyorker.com/news/news-desk/two-connecticut-school-districts-for-the-rich-and-poor. See also "Connecticut—Education and Opportunity," Realize the Dream, http://www.realizethedream.org/reports/states/connecticut.html; and Rebecca Klein, "Connecticut Makes Rare Progress on School Segregation as America Moves Backwards," *HuffPost*, May 15, 2015, https://www.huffingtonpost.com/2015/05/15/connecticut-school-desegregation_n_7269750.html.
5. Hannah Arendt, *Eichmann in Jerusalem: A Report on the Banality of Evil* (1963; reprint New York, NY: Penguin, 2006).

Chapter 6: The Rotation of the Earth

1. Katie Nodjimbadem, "The Long, Painful History of Police Brutality in the U.S.," *Smithsonian*, July 27, 2017, https://www.smithsonianmag.com/smithsonian-institution/long-painful-history-police-brutality-in-the-us-180964098/.
2. "Assessing The $100 Million Upheaval of Newark's Public Schools," September 21, 2015, NPR (heard on *Fresh Air*), https://www.npr.org/2015/09/21/442183080/assessing-the-100-million-upheaval-of-newarks-public-schools.

3. "Poverty Rate, by Race and Ethnicity, Nativity, and Citizenship Status, 1973–2013" (chart), The State of Working America, accessed April 2, 2018, http://www.stateofworkingamerica.org/chart/swa-poverty-figure-7c-poverty-rate-raceethnicity/.
4. "U.S. Poverty Statistics," Federal Safety Net, accessed February 6, 2018, http://federalsafetynet.com/us-poverty-statistics.html.
5. "Status and Trends in the Education of Racial and Ethnic Groups 2016," National Center for Education Statistics, August 2016, page v, https://nces.ed.gov/pubs2016/2016007.pdf.
6. "Unemployment Rates by Age, Sex, Race, and Hispanic or Latino Ethnicity," Bureau of Labor Statistics, last modified January 5, 2018, table E-16, https://www.bls.gov/web/empsit/cpsee_e16.htm.
7. Eileen Patten, "Racial, Gender Wage Gaps Persist in U.S. Despite Some Progress," Pew Research Center, July 1, 2016, http://www.pewresearch.org/fact-tank/2016/07/01/racial-gender-wage-gaps-persist-in-u-s-despite-some-progress/.

Chapter 7: Insidious Irony

1. Charles Duhigg, *The Power of Habit: Why We Do What We Do in Life and Business* (New York: Random House, 2014).
2. Tom Shatel, "The Unknown Barry Switzer: Poverty, Tragedy Built Oklahoma Coach into a Winner," *Chicago Tribune*, December 14, 1986, http://articles.chicagotribune.com/1986-12-14/sports/8604030680_1_big-eight-coach-aren-t-many-coaches-oklahoma.
3. Suniya S. Luthar, "The Culture of Affluence: Psychological Costs of Material Wealth," *Child Development* 74, no. 6 (2003): 1581–93, https://www.ncbi.nlm.nih.gov/pmc/articles/PMC1950124/.
4. Steve Crabtree and Brett Pelham, "Religion Provides Emotional Boost to World's Poor," *Gallup News*, March 6, 2009, http://news.gallup.com/poll/116449/religion-provides-emotional-boost-world-poor.aspx.
5. David Masci, "How Income Varies among U.S. Religious Groups," Pew Research Center, October 11, 2016, http://www.pewresearch.org/fact-tank/2016/10/11/how-income-varies-among-u-s-religious-groups/.
6. Madeline Levine, *The Price of Privilege: How Parental Pressure and Material Advantage are Creating a Generation of Disconnected and Unhappy Kids* (New York, NY: HarperCollins, 2006), 14.
7. Jeffrey M. Jones, "Drinking Highest among Educated, Upper-Income Americans," *Gallup News*, July 27, 2015, http://news.gallup.com/poll/184358/drinking-highest-among-educated-upper-income-americans.aspx.
8. Megan E. Patrick et al., "Socioeconomic Status and Substance Use among

Young Adults: A Comparison across Constructs and Drugs," *Journal of Studies on Alcohol and Drugs* 73, no. 5 (Sep 2012): 772–82, https://www.ncbi.nlm.nih.gov/pmc/articles/PMC3410945/.

9. Hara Estroff Marano, "Teens: Suburban Blues," *Psychology Today*, March 22, 2005, last reviewed June 9, 2016, https://www.psychologytoday.com/us/articles/200503/teens-suburban-blues. See also Suniya S. Luthar, "The Problem with Rich Kids," *Psychology Today*, November 5, 2013, last reviewed June 9, 2016, https://www.psychologytoday.com/us/articles/201311/the-problem-rich-kids.
10. Luke 12:22-34.
11. To learn about Maslow's hierarchy of needs, see Saul McLeod, "Maslow's Hierarchy of Needs," *Simply Psychology*, updated 2017, https://www.simplypsychology.org/maslow.html.

Chapter 8: Blessed

1. I tell this story at the beginning of *A Good and Perfect Gift: Faith, Expectations, and a Little Girl Named Penny* (Grand Rapids: Baker, 2011).
2. Genesis 18:18.
3. Matthew 5:13.
4. Romans 8:28.
5. Marianne Bertrand and Sendhil Mullainathan, "Are Emily and Greg More Employable Than Lakisha and Jamal? A Field Experiment On Labor Market Discrimination," NBER Working Paper Series, National Bureau of Economic Research, Cambridge, MA, Working Paper 9873, July 2003, http://www.nber.org/papers/w9873.pdf.

Chapter 9: Looking Up

1. John 14:3.
2. John 10:10.
3. Revelation 21:4.
4. Luke 23:43.

Chapter 10: Beloved

1. Olga Khazan, "Remembering the Nazis' Disabled Victims," *The Atlantic*, September 3, 2014, https://www.theatlantic.com/health/archive/2014/09/a-memorial-to-the-nazis-disabled-victims/379528/.
2. Joseph Shapiro, "The Sexual Assault Epidemic No One Talks About," *NPR News*, January 8, 2018, https://www.npr.org/2018/01/08/570224090/the-sexual-assault-epidemic-no-one-talks-about.

3. Genesis 1:27.
4. 1 John 4:8.
5. Genesis 3.

Chapter 11: Possibilities

1. Rasheed Malik, "New Data Reveal 250 Preschoolers Are Suspended or Expelled Every Day," Center for American Progress, November 6, 2017, https://www.americanprogress.org/issues/early-childhood/news/2017/11/06/442280/new-data-reveal-250-preschoolers-suspended-expelled-every-day/.
2. Kimberly Hively and Amani El-Alayli, "'You Throw Like a Girl': The Effect of Stereotype Threat on Women's Athletic Performance and Gender Stereotypes," *Psychology of Sport and Exercise* 15, no. 1 (January 2014): 48–55, http://www.sciencedirect.com/science/article/pii/S1469029213000861.
3. Linda Wertheimer, "A Final Word with President's Faithful Speechwriter," *NPR Morning Edition*, June 21, 2006, https://www.npr.org/templates/story/story.php?storyId=5499701. The phrase was included in a speech Gerson wrote for President George W. Bush, delivered to the NAACP July 10, 2000, http://www.washingtonpost.com/wp-srv/onpolitics/elections/bushtext071000.htm.
4. Carol S. Dweck, *Mindset: The New Psychology of Success* (New York: Ballantine Books, 2016). For a concise visual summary of Dweck's work, see http://bit.ly/2IMrCV0.
5. Christopher de Vinck, *Power of the Powerless: A Brother's Legacy of Love* (New York: Doubleday, 1988), 9.
6. Gregory Boyle, *Tattoos on the Heart: The Power of Boundless Compassion* (New York: Free Press, 2010); and Gregory Boyle, *Barking to the Choir: The Power of Radical Kinship* (New York: Simon & Schuster, 2017).
7. Michael Longley, "The Vitality of Ordinary Things," interview by Krista Tippett, *On Being*, November 3, 2016, https://onbeing.org/programs/michael-longley-the-vitality-of-ordinary-things/.
8. Philippians 1:9.
9. Galatians 5:6.
10. Ephesians 3:19.
11. 1 Corinthians 13:2.

Chapter 12: Necessary Action

1. Ephesians 3:17-18.

Chapter 13: To Act Justly

1. Luke 11:3, KJV.
2. Zechariah 7:9.
3. Psalm 33:5.
4. Isaiah 30:18.

Chapter 14: A Reversal

1. John 5:5-9
2. Ta-Nehisi Coates, "The Case for Reparations," *The Atlantic*, June 2014, https://www.theatlantic.com/magazine/archive/2014/06/the-case-for-reparations/361631/.
3. D. L. Mayfield, "Cover Story: Facing Our Legacy of Lynching," *Christianity Today*, August 18, 2017, http://www.christianitytoday.com/ct/2017/september/legacy-lynching-america-christians-repentance.html.

About the Author

Amy Julia Becker graduated from Princeton University with a master's degree in English literature and a certificate in African American studies. She received a master of divinity degree from Princeton Theological Seminary. In addition to her numerous articles for online and print publication, she has authored three other books. *Small Talk: Learning from My Children about What Matters Most* is a parenting memoir about the spiritual growth that can happen in the midst of the challenges of having young children. The award-winning *A Good and Perfect Gift: Faith, Expectations, and a Little Girl Named Penny* is a spiritual memoir about how Amy Julia confronted her own perfectionism and came to receive Penny as a gift after she was diagnosed with Down syndrome. *Penelope Ayers* is a memoir about hope in the face of loss as Amy Julia cared for her mother-in-law after her diagnosis of liver cancer. Learn more and find resources related to *White Picket Fences* at www.amyjuliabecker.com.

THE NAVIGATORS® STORY

THANK YOU for picking up this NavPress book! I hope it has been a blessing to you.

NavPress is a ministry of The Navigators. The Navigators began in the 1930s, when a young California lumberyard worker named Dawson Trotman was impacted by basic discipleship principles and felt called to teach those principles to others. He saw this mission as an echo of 2 Timothy 2:2: "And the things you have heard me say in the presence of many witnesses entrust to reliable people who will also be qualified to teach others" (NIV).

In 1933, Trotman and his friends began discipling members of the US Navy. By the end of World War II, thousands of men on ships and bases around the world were learning the principles of spiritual multiplication by the intentional, person-to-person teaching of God's Word.

After World War II, The Navigators expanded its relational ministry to include college campuses; local churches; the Glen Eyrie Conference Center and Eagle Lake Camps in Colorado Springs, Colorado; and neighborhood and citywide initiatives across the country and around the world.

Today, with more than 2,600 US staff members—and local ministries in more than 100 countries—The Navigators continues the transformational process of making disciples who make more disciples, advancing the Kingdom of God in a world that desperately needs the hope and salvation of Jesus Christ and the encouragement to grow deeper in relationship with Him.

NAVPRESS was created in 1975 to advance the calling of The Navigators by bringing biblically rooted and culturally relevant products to people who want to know and love Christ more deeply. In January 2014, NavPress entered an alliance with Tyndale House Publishers to strengthen and better position our rich content for the future. Through *THE MESSAGE* Bible and other resources, NavPress seeks to bring positive spiritual movement to people's lives.

If you're interested in learning more or becoming involved with The Navigators, go to www.navigators.org. For more discipleship content from The Navigators and NavPress authors, visit www.thedisciplemaker.org. May God bless you in your walk with Him!

Sincerely,

DON PAPE
VP/PUBLISHER, NAVPRESS